THE SINS OF THE JUST

"For a just man shall fall seven times and shall rise again; but the wicked shall fall down into evil" (Prv 24:16).

"If we say we have no sin, we deceive ourselves and the truth is not in us" (1 Jn 1:8).

The SINS of the JUST

✝

By John H. McGoey, S.F.M.

THE BRUCE PUBLISHING COMPANY
Milwaukee

IMPRIMI POTEST:

Francis M. Diemert, S.F.M.
Superior General

NIHIL OBSTAT:
John F. Murphy, S.T.D.
Censor librorum

IMPRIMATUR:
✝ William E. Cousins
Archbishop of Milwaukee
February 27, 1963

Library of Congress Catalog Card Number: 63–14922

(Second Printing — 1963)

Contents

v

THE SINS OF THE JUST

1. The Problem

RELIGIOUS are publicly dedicated to the imitation of Jesus Christ in thought, word, and deed. Their way of life should be the greatest, most rewarding in the world. Leading to God, it should be simple. In practice it is not. Many are surprised and disappointed that holiness does not drop on them like the mantle of Elias. Mastering self is a hard process. Spiritual exercises do not develop the soul as physical exercises do the body. Holiness sought begets pride oftener than union with God. Time in religion cannot be equated with spirituality nor does it make sanctity inevitable. The many, complicated explanations of these facts are beyond the scope of this book. Its theme is that religious life is meaningless if the image of Christ is not etched in the nun's soul, and Christ more manifest to the world by her life.

Since unity with Christ is the heart of the spiritual life, sharing in His passion is necessarily the lot of the religious. "If anyone will come after me, let him pick up his cross and follow me." Acceptance of the invitation is a pledge of the will to conquer self. Consent to walk in the footsteps of Christ means the will to root out pride. Pride, ego, selfishness are the only genuine obstacles to holiness. No rule of life can confer it, nor is one religious order more successful than another in leading its members to it. Any way of life is itself lifeless. God alone gives life as well as the increase of life which is holiness.

Holiness is not for the nun who thinks or believes she has abandoned herself to the designs of God, but for the nun who has actually left her life in His hands. The problem is to come to grips with self, to love Christ as He wishes rather than in the way she chooses. God, not self, must be the object of her affections. Christ is THE RULE for religious, Christ as He is found in the Gospels. In the Gospels too is found the best formula for holiness. It is John the Baptist's. He summed up all that matters when he said so simply and profoundly, "He must increase; I must decrease." The spiritual books of the world can be searched from cover to cover in vain for a clearer definition of the secret of sanctity.

Glorification of the community rule, the stressing of its reading, the respect due it, or dedication to God through following constitutions is worse than useless unless the Gospel Christ is ever before the eyes of the religious. The further she gets away from this simple fact, the further she escapes her only problem, self, and her only answer, God.

The first part of this book draws in lines much too faint the Christ of the Passion, the One who loves His religious more than anyone else could love her. This is to encourage her to accept everything in life that likens her to Him. The second part is a criticism of religious and religious life. It may well be negative and even hypercritical but it may also help the religious to see herself more truly. It should help her to understand what religious life could and should be. Certainly the nun's desire to improve is the measure of her love for God, IF it is for God that she wants to be perfect in the first place.

A priest sits in the confessional. A penitent confesses that he blasphemed, missed Mass, beat his wife and children, committed adultery, robbed a bank, and destroyed the good name of his neighbor. The priest need not be a profound theologian to conclude that the penitent should not do these things. It is not difficult to recognize the sins of the wicked. They are obvious, admitted, and sometimes regretted. Not so the sins of the just. These are seldom obvious to the sinner, let alone the confessor. They are rarely admitted and almost never regretted. Yet these sins set the limits of the spiritual progress of the just. And when these limits are reached the things of God turn to dust and ashes in the mouth of the just religious. Although she may see how pointless would be a return to the world, to continue the travesty of religious life seems even more pointless. This is not the dark night of the soul in which the religious feels no joy or consolation in her life. In the dark night she retains her taste for the things of God; she simply does not experience their sweetness.

How does a young woman, wishing to give herself to God without reserve, come to this pass?

First, she just does not know how to give unreservedly. Like the young bride she does not clearly understand what is involved in her promises. While saying "for better, for worse," she expects only the better. For her, "richer or poorer" means only richer. "In sickness and health" to the young and healthy is without real significance. Few Catholic brides making their vows look much beyond the present. Religious making their vows are not much different.

Second, she is so human, and so few humans can love truly. Yet Christ's invitation to His followers is to love truly. The real obstacles to this love are the sins of the just, the kind that are committed seven times a day and hardly noticed. The sins of the just take away the taste for the things of God. They lead the nun to believe her Lord is long acoming, to be impatient for her freedom, her pleasure, and her joy.

Third, religious have been frequently misled. It is no small thing to speak in the name of God. It should be done sparingly, with great diffidence. But the spokesmen for God too quickly discourage attention to the direct work of God in the soul through grace, in favor of the apparently safer course, the written and the spoken word. Yet God never ceases working directly in the soul by grace. If a woman's very fingerprints distinguish her from every other living soul how much more distinguished is she by the graces which are God's gift to her alone.

There is a morbid fear in most religious of becoming stray sheep. To avoid this they tend to forsake their individuality. The Good Shepherd said, "I know mine and mine know me." Christ does not love souls in mobs or herds or flocks, but each in her own way, to her own capacity, to the degree of her abandonment to Him. In rejection of her selfness rather than her selfishness, the religious loses sight of this.

Living for God is much more than avoiding blasphemy and other serious offenses against Him. It is giving one's life to God in very deed. The entire purpose of the nun in placing her life in the hands of God is that He, knowing all things and able to do all things, will direct that life unerringly to its ultimate destiny. It is accomplished by allowing Him the freedom He wants to do in the soul the work that He alone can do. Her life could be in no better hands; none knows better what she needs or how to fulfill those needs than the God who made her.

When a religious gives her soul to God in a public profession of vows and then begins little by little to take that life back into her own control, she voids the very authority she has given God to help her. This "little by little" is nothing but the sins of the just. The confessor regrets the failure of the sinner to appreciate what she is missing by her life in sin. But the priest dealing with souls pledged to the spiritual life is in anguish when the sins of the just deprive them of the joy of their vocation. These sins are legion and all religious suffer from them more or less. They do not kill the soul but they slowly paralyze it. No religious is more surely the victim of them than the nun who has given her life to God with her mouth but withheld it from her heart.

2. *The Essence of Life in Christ*

ST. PAUL was in labor over his Christians until Christ was formed in them. If St. Paul's yearnings and tireless efforts were to this end what is the will of Christ for the religious? She is to walk the path He walked. She will learn from the Passion where and through what that path leads. In all that lies ahead, her understanding of the Passion assures her all the help she needs to do what has to be done. If her religious life begins with the words "Into Thy hands I commend my spirit," it will end with Christ's words too, "It is consummated." The joys of Christ's Resurrection are inseparable from the pains of His Passion, but anticipation of a joy so palatable easily blots out the thorny approach to it. The lessons of the Passion are inexhaustible. They are also indispensable.

As Christ stood, hands tied, before Pilate He was officially and formally rejected by mankind, by the world. He took flesh, proved His divinity by word and by work, and challenged men to be good. And men, as they so often do, refused to adjust their lives to meet that challenge. To save face they had to reject and dispose of the Challenger. Christ was rejected. Of this there is no doubt. Yet religious clearly expect to be praised and respected because of their state. In fact, all too often they demand respect. Christ before them was rejected without complaint while mere criticism is intolerable to His "chosen" souls. Incongruously the religious self-righteously spurns the very rejection which would make her the companion of Christ.

Nor can a religious claim that Christ promised anything but rejection. "The disciple is not more worthy than the Master." "If they have done this to me they shall also do it to you." Nor was this rejection to lead anywhere but to Calvary and the Cross. The Apostles were rebuked time and again for not savoring the things which were to their good; for preferring the road to earthly glory and to primacy. Peter's protest to Christ about His trip to Jerusalem to suffer and to die brought forth Christ's stinging identification of him with the devil, "Get thou behind me, Satan." How well those words cover religious who insist that they seek only dignity and glory for the Church while being the first to relish its pomp and pageantry. Persecution and suffering have seldom threatened the Mystical Body as seriously as have power and prestige. The world's contempt for religious has ruined fewer of them than has its embrace. Religious are mistaken when without consciously doing so they overlook the rejection promised them by Christ. This oversight is evident when poverty, chastity, and obedience have become matter for legal arbitration rather than the obvious virtues of the followers of Christ. Those who exercise authority in the name of Christ have no choice but to exemplify the virtues of Christ. The religious who does not share His rejection hardly shares His virtues.

Christ before Pilate was a strange sight. Christ the Judge, God, innocent, stood judged before Pilate, man, guilty. Without protest He heard Himself condemned to die unjustly. Since man, creature, through his proud defiance of

God, closed the gates of heaven against himself, Christ, God, would through His humble obedience to man be crucified to open those gates. Surely this should make the religious think. It is more than ample explanation of any injustice she could suffer. The religious superior should consider the effrontery of Pilate wielding his authority to punish the innocent in the name of law and order. The religious subject should see the incongruity of insisting on her innocence when the innocent Christ accepted punishment without protest.

Physical suffering is less a stumbling block to the religious than suffering injustice. Standing before the first station of the cross she should find sufficient explanation unless her mind is completely preoccupied with self. Too often the religious must see some justice in her suffering before it is acceptable to her. She may foolishly try to convince herself that she deserves what she is receiving or that the one punishing her does so unknowingly. Surely the fact that Christ before her suffered unjustly, that the disciple is not more worthy than the Master, should make her lot not only acceptable but comprehensible. "Where I am there also shall my servant be" does not refer only to heaven. "If they have done these things in the green wood what shall be done in the dry?" "I send you as sheep before wolves . . . those that persecute you and put you to death shall think they are rendering a service to God."

Legal spirituality creates the theology of minimums. The fulfillment of the least required amount, doing the bare necessities, establishing the lowest average for entering the kingdom of heaven, seeking to have one's cake and eat it too — these are the factors in the theology of minimums. Since a religious is forbidden to keep money in her cell, she will keep it under a brick on her windowsill. Since a religious cannot have a car, she will arrange for her family to take her where she wants to go (often regardless of the inconvenience or scandal to them). She makes plans for a prepaid vacation and then inspires the generous benefactor to seek permission for it. Her theology permits any luxury paid for by the laity; it sets prudent limits to the efforts she must make for souls and God. Yet she does not find it strange that the God of theology in His redemption of man chose the extravagance of crucifixion as a criminal.

The crucifix has become a glorious Christian symbol; it stood for utter ignominy when Christ died upon it. Such a death was too much for the lowest Roman citizen guilty of the most despicable of crimes. Yet it was acceptable to the Son of God. The reason He chose so to die was simply His unfathomable love for man. Religious life is reasonable only in total dedication, complete abandonment to God with minimal thought of self. Trust in God cannot come from the theology of minimums but only from deep faith in the Gospels. "If your children ask for bread, do you give them a stone? If they ask for a fig, do you give them a scorpion? If then you know how to give good gifts to your children, how much more does your heavenly Father provide for his children?" (Luke 11:11–13.) If the crucifix worn as part of the religious garb does not represent her abandonment to God, her willingness to be crucified with Christ, it were better torn off and thrown away.

Yet only the most realistic nun believes this; it is considered by the others pious fervor, something over and above what has been asked despite the Gospel insistence on it. Little wonder, then, that those who justify their partial following of Christ by legalism, pseudo prudence, or the "practical" interpretation of Christ have only partial happiness in their lives rather than the hundredfold promised by Christ to those who go all the way. The Gospels are certainly clear about this. The watering down of the message of Christ is just a sop to those wishing, like the rich young man, to be perfect without selling what they have, giving it to the poor, and following Christ. Many religious rejoice in the vows of poverty, chastity, and obedience without actually selling their goods, without detachment, without docility. Regardless of legal justification they ignore the Gospel. Therefore they can and should expect nothing more than a partial reward, a partial happiness, a vague, cloudy image of Christ in their souls.

The Gospels have been enshrined for centuries as sacred books containing the holy and inspired word of God. Ordinary people are apt to miss the implications of them in their daily lives. Unfortunately, so also does the average religious. So many things about the life of Christ the normal nun feels she will never be required to imitate or experience, yet it is her privilege to follow Christ right to the crucifixion, the death of self. Because she is nailed by the will of others to a duty she does not like, on a hill she does not wish to climb, through a judgment she thinks unjust, she resists the obvious conclusion.

Many are oblivious to certain features of the falls of Christ along the road. What normal person at the roadside could have, without divine revelation, believed for a moment that the man lying in the filthy street was actually the Son of God? Who could ever have seen in the bloodstained, dirty face, borne to the ground by the felon's burden of the cross, the Son of God redeeming mankind? The answer is, simply, no one. What was happening was beyond human comprehension. Surely no one who could avoid such a thing would willingly accept it. But the nun does know the truth. She does know Who lay in the dirt of the streets of Jerusalem that Good Friday. But in spite of her knowledge and all that He Himself has said to that effect, does she understand that such must be her fate? The answer is, just as simply and truly, no. She is as blind to her destiny as were the passersby to the identity of the Criminal crushed before them under His cross. Through too many dramatic portrayals the crucifixion of Christ is not quite real. The fact of Christ's suffering and death has been accepted, but it has not been identified with the crucifixion of self required of every religious if she is to rise again with Christ.

Something of this can be understood in contemplating Christ face to face with His Mother. Saccharine spirituality has obscured much of the truth expressed in this meeting. Certainly Mary was never involved for a moment in the guilt of sin which brought suffering to her Son. She was innocent; she was, on the testimony of the angel, full of grace. Yet more than any human being she participated in the sufferings of Christ. It is almost incomprehensible that Christ loving her so could have permitted her such suffering. Surely it is the way of love to spare the beloved. But if Mary's love for God meant anything, it meant oneness of mind and heart with her Son. And that oneness demanded that the depths of her suffering be second only to her Son's. It was her privilege, as it is the privilege of the religious to a lesser degree, to be one with Him in suffering. Only had He loved His Mother less could He have refused her permission to be one with Him in this horrible undertaking. He has promised religious, too, the joy of being with Him in His greatest moments, those in which He is dying for

men. "For this cause was I born and for this came I into
the world." The sense of privilege keeps the religious, as it
kept His Mother, from uttering a word of complaint. The
difficulty for the religious, despite Christ's clarity of teaching, is to see in the suffering of this moment any relationship
to the Passion of Christ. It is part of the suffering that it can
be accepted on faith alone.

Christ is crucified daily and His religious is crucified daily
with Him, if she loves Him. But this love demands that two
extremes be avoided. She must not plead to be spared the
suffering that is her destiny unless she wants to deprive
herself of the choicest graces. On the other hand, she must
never make a virtue of suffering in itself. Too often the
religious is shocked to realize that she is pledged to suffering; too seldom is she detached enough from self to realize
that suffering of itself is without merit. Virtue, of course, lies
in the middle way. The struggle for the middle road takes
place between the poles of hopelessness and joy. Persever-
ance in it brings the greatest victory of all, conquest of self.

Souls sometimes wrestle with the problem of suffering to
their own destruction. After offering their lives to God they
recoil at the specter of suffering. It is not so much today
they fear as the whole long life ahead of them. They can
neither live a day at a time nor understand that love never
demands the impossible. Their fear of the future prevents
them from crediting God with supplying the strength needed
just when it is needed. Other souls are ambitious, aspiring to
true holiness which they see as the only real greatness. They
reach the point where they see the road to glory in suffering.
But, almost unknown to them it is their own glory they
aspire to. They make a fetish of suffering; they are com-
placent in it. The value of everything is estimated by the

amount of suffering involved. Their preoccupation with suffering becomes morbid. Anyone but they who pursue it with such singleness of purpose can see it as unhealthy, twisted, and perverted. The suffering quickly becomes the suffering of their choice, selected with poor discernment rather than accepted from Divine Providence, the Shaper of souls.

Such a nun is more to be pitied than the lax one. She is the last to see the true object of her suffering, her own glory, her own sanctification without much reference to God. In the final analysis she ludicrously pits her planning against God's, so intent is she on painting her own picture. How logical that the work is amateurish, the ravages of the process astounding. The Mother of Christ suffered, but to the exact degree and in the exact way that God willed. There was nothing of the self-made martyr in her; no paranoidal misery of soul. Her suffering was objective, true, and efficacious. To suffer with Christ one must develop the emotional control necessary to restrict pain to its proper place, within its proper limits, enduring what must be suffered without self-pity. An understanding of Mary's suffering should eliminate both presumption and fear in the approach of the religious to suffering. It restricts her to that willed by God and protects her from the flattery of suffering sought.

The extent of Christ's rejection is plain. None of the beneficiaries of His material or spiritual largess was willing to share His burden. Where were the lepers, the blind, the lame, and the possessed? Simon of Cyrene had to be forced to accept what every succeeding generation knew to be the greatest of privileges. But it certainly was not the lame and the blind and the other unfortunates who caused Christ the greatest disappointment at this time. It was the Apostles, who not only received His gifts but even shared His presence and His power. And they had no other excuse for their flight than their humanity. Having seen what they saw and heard what they heard, this day would remain a disgrace to them throughout all time. For the more honest religious this scene is a haunting reminder of their early aspirations and a disappointing picture of their accomplishments. The not-so-honest religious remain convinced that had they been present they would have given a better account of themselves than did the Apostles. Who can say they are wrong? Yet, through neglect of the reading of the Gospel, religious can still overlook the words, "As long as you did it not for one of these my least brethren you did it not for me."

And so one sister can refuse to talk to another, or pass by when she is in need, or forget her obligations in charity to those she deals with daily in her work. Sadly, many people see precious little of Christ in the religious supervising them. While destiny did not find religious standing along the road to Calvary two thousand years ago, they are not thereby deprived of the same opportunity. Few have paid more dearly than religious for this oversight. For not only is Christ less a force in their lives but they lack the stimulus of remorse to make up for their omissions. The nun who does not see Christ every day in those around her has all but ceased to believe in Christ; her life is close to being the highest form of folly.

Many of the most effective fighters of modern war are not in uniform; they are heroes whose only insignia is bravery and their willingness to be forgotten in the victory they hope for. In the war against sin there are countless religious in their habits reminding the passersby that they are professionally dedicated to the love of Christ. Yet many a simple washerwoman spends more time contemplating than some contemplatives, many a mother is a more dedicated teacher than some religious in the university, many a worker in the factory a more eloquent preacher than some pulpit orators, and many parents far more dedicated than some pastors.

So it was with the woman named Veronica. Not a queen, nor elsewhere mentioned in the Gospels, nor even listed among the women ministering to Jesus and the Apostles, yet this woman is destined never to be forgotten where the name of Jesus is mentioned. Like Magdalen it was her love alone which made her place in history. It did not matter to her that every face but the Cyrene's was hostile to Christ; it did not matter that she would be scorned or even trampled in anger to the ground, or torn to shreds by the demented mob engaged in deicide. It was Christ who mattered. Alone, blinded by sweat and blood, exhausted by sleeplessness, hunger, thirst, and hemorrhage, He seemed abandoned even by God. Bound by no vow to do so she went to Him regardless of everything, pressed on by a love which would not be restrained.

Surely the religious can see here the casting out of the children of the kingdom and the invitation to the gentiles; surely she can see the emptiness of the religious garb without love in it. While the habit does not make the monk, love does make the religious. Sharing the Passion does mark that love. It were better for a religious never to have been born than to have been professed unconvinced of this. If these notions are hard they belong to Christ. Those who have the ambition to sit on His right and His left in the kingdom of heaven had better be prepared also to drink of His chalice.

Religious life is so arranged as to free its subjects from much of the uncertainty, trial, and anguish of the world that they might seek a high degree of union with God in prayer. However, this exemption from the worries of the world can be used to relax and live their lives to suit themselves. The religious who know what they should be but are not prepared to pay the cost, and even demand immunity from the cost in the name of God, are pharisees, before whom even the publicans and harlots will go into heaven.

The agony of Christ was enough to kill Him several times had He been subject to sickness and to death. But He was not. "I take my life up and I lay it down again," He said. We cannot be sure of the historicity of the three falls of Christ but early tradition had it that there were three. Certainly it is reasonable to assume there were. They make the extreme of His suffering more obvious. Religious need to see Christ fall again and again and pick Himself up and go on when He had neither heart nor taste for doing so. There are times in religious life when everything in one cries out for the end of it. There is no nun opening herself to the work of God in her soul, watching her own resources dwindle, her complacency erased, her taste for the things of God dried up, her personality absorbed in anonymity, her deepest aspirations confused even in her own mind with pride and arrogance, who does not need to see Christ fall helpless in the road only to rise and go on again.

Christ speaking to the women of Jerusalem illustrates a virtue which the nun in her career needs far more than others: selflessness, forgetfulness of self. The women of Christ's time lived in a cruel world. They were accustomed to replacing beasts of burden in the fields. Brutality was no stranger to them; they could accept things as routine which would make moderns turn away with revulsion and disgust. Yet the pitiable state of Christ compelled their tears. It could have been the normal woman's compassion at the plight of the most beautiful of the children of men. It may have been that these women were the beneficiaries of Christ's power to heal or help, and they were grateful at least to the point of tears. Still none had more right to feel sorry for himself at this point than did Christ. He had no reason to be where He was but the love for ungrateful man; His very life was hanging only by the thread of His own power. A single moment of consent and He would suffer no more. Yet not even for that split second did His concern leave the people who needed pity more than He. "Weep not for me but for yourselves and for your children," He said. Who but Almighty God could have felt like that at such a time. What an example for the religious wallowing in the bogs of self-pity!

When for the best of reasons one is exempted from the normal cares of a home and family it is easy to become too concerned with self. Petty troubles can become major afflictions. Sometimes a skilled physician cannot tell whether the sufferings of religious are of the body or of the mind. Doctors are deeply baffled at times by the failure of religious to rely on the omnipotent God to whom they are vowed. Like the Apostles they fear for their lives while Christ is still in the boat. There are religious so solicitous for self that, blind to thousands of less fortunates around them enduring far greater things without complaint, they live almost as souls without hope, beyond help.

A life of continuous self-scrutiny is not pleasant. For the victim of self-pity it is impossible. The obstacles to virtue seem insurmountable to her and the resources with which she is to meet the challenge always seem inadequate. She either fears that God will ask the impossible or doubts that

His resources are available to her. On the other hand, the religious whose mind is on God knows that all things are possible with Him and that He is lavish with the graces required to do what He asks. To her, anxiety lest she fail is understandable; lack of trust is not.

Pride is the root of all evil, and humiliation its expiation. Nowhere along the road could Christ's atonement for the pride of men be more candidly portrayed than in His stripping. Public stripping for a public figure is a form of acute torture. Many prefer suicide to facing it. It made the power of God in Christ look pathetic. Even when Herod made a clown of Him He was at least dressed. When they had exhausted every other humiliation they stripped Him, and when this was done there was only one other thing to do, and that was to die. Christ would not permit Himself the luxury of death until He had suffered the ultimate. Through this as through His other humiliations He was showing what power could come to men by His example, the power to overcome themselves and their pride.

But man, it seems, can overcome the whole world before conquering himself. Yet there is no higher form of greatness for man than mastery of self. His eternal life depends on it. What man unwilling to be stripped of his clothes is willing to be stripped of his pride by having his sins exposed? Such a man believes he is greater than God. The proud strut of the worldling should not be the gait of the follower of Christ. Those in authority, those so conscious that they act in the name of God, should be the first to admit their mistakes, to seek help in their decisions, to understand their limitations. Too often, blinded by pride, they plead that they would be letting the Church down in admitting they had erred when in truth the scandal is in failing to do so. Surely in being stripped naked on Calvary Christ was especially atoning for the pride and arrogance of those using religious life for their own glory, reveling in the perquisites of office, loving dignities and honors which many an honest worldling would be ashamed to accept.

Expecting the fate of her Master, the religious is nevertheless stunned when she experiences it. The world which hated Him is only now hating her. Raised in a home where religion was esteemed and religious venerated, she let His warning pass unnoticed. It did not make sense. Sin never makes sense. Why should hands be tied which work no evil? Or feet restrained which walk only on missions of peace or mercy? And this while the hand raised in anger remains unchecked and the feet walking in darkness pass uncensured. Mystified, she watches the wayward having her paths smoothed while the course of the devoted is strewn with obstacles. This confusion is resolved or compounded for the religious just insofar as she subscribes to Christ's way or the world's. Christ permitted Himself to be nailed to the cross. He did not ask for it or avoid it, bring it on Himself or fly from it. He accepted the chalice to be drunk by those destined to sit at the right hand and the left.

The world will not be diverted from its course. The religious daring to remind that world by their lives that there is more to be sought in life than pleasure, can expect to hear the same verdict, "Let them be crucified." Man's burden of gratitude to Christ was too much for him to bear. He revolted and crucified Him. The same fate should hardly come as a surprise to a religious. That the crucifixion is of soul rather than body undoubtedly explains the confusion; but the fact that it is perpetrated by the chosen ones of God should clarify it. Again, if the religious finds correction hard to take, how impossible is it for the world to accept it; how logical that the rebuke of a good life should be repaid with crucifixion.

The nun must be careful not to look on her crucifixion as a proof of her election. The world is more intolerant of the hypocrite than it is of the saint, and Christ agreed with the world in His disdain for hypocrisy. The pharisee at prayer was not rebuked because he lied in listing his virtuous acts. He did these things. His performance was revolting because his purpose was his own glory not God's. Much of the persecution of religious is brought upon themselves. The publicity of their communities and organizations sent out by their own offices for their own glory disgusts more than it edifies. It contributes very little to the one job of the religious, development through the grace of God of the image of Christ in her own soul and the souls of others. Crucified for this she is a martyr; crucified for hypocrisy she is the victim of her own press releases. A religious who is considered holy gives pause for thought when this reputation can be traced back to her own revelation of it, "in the strictest confidence, of course," to a friend.

The climax of the spiritual life is the death of the religious in the manner of the Master, with forgiveness on her lips. The mark of Christ is on the religious who always forgives. "Not seven times, but until seventy times seven times," He said. "If you love your friends, what is this? For even the heathens do this. But I say, love your enemies." The ability to do this merits the certificate of Christian maturity.

There is the height of isolation in the death of Christ. He was alone, terribly alone. The necessary loneliness of religious life enables the nun to share this loneliness of Christ. The prospect of a lonely death cannot strike terror in the heart of one who has accepted the loneliness of life. The nun should not rejoice in being friendless but she should be able to live by herself. Desolation is part of the redemptive process. The thought of it makes even the strong tremble. Christ Himself shrank from it. But — a vital point in the nun's life — it represents the precise moment when she is separated from herself. Her consent to the isolation of abandonment marks the complete acceptance of God's plan for her. It must always remain emotionally revolting to her even when her mind and will give full and comprehending acceptance to it. It is possible only for the religious whose understanding prevails over her emotions.

Christ asked nothing but faith and trust of the Apostles when they were beset by dangers. This is all He asks of His religious. Many times she comes to the point where she must either trust or turn back. Most religious naturally prefer to stop there. The next step is too frightening, inevitable though it is. Since it is inevitable, not a moment's hesitation should be permitted. If, trusting in God and relying on His unlimited resources, the step is taken, the soul's abandonment to God can well be final.

There is peace and tranquillity in acceptance of the death of Christ. For regardless of the anguish, the course is run, the debt is completely paid. The religious can expect the same peace and tranquillity in her own death if she has faith. For her, too, the course will then be run and the cause won. She really believed the invitation to follow Christ. It was not just an edifying or poetic thing meant in an accommodated or metaphorical sense, a spiritually synthetic spur to her immature enthusiasm for religion. It was real. How real she will only know fully in eternity but some of its reality she can grasp before that. Only a Jansenistic insistence on unworthiness prevents her grasp of it. She does not doubt the reality of religious life; no more should she doubt the possibility of following Christ literally, truly.

There is less psychological penalty for accepting Christ entirely or rejecting Him entirely than there is for the half measure. Half-dedicated lives have neither the spiritual exaltation of the fulfilled nor the comfortable relaxation of the genuinely indifferent. A dull emptiness is the lot of those who cannot go all out until they have more assurance of the quick benefits of the venture. They hold back the gift of themselves to God, terrified at the prospect of suffering, only to suffer terror at the thought of sacrificing ultimate happiness.

After Christ's death the emphasis moves from Him to His Mother. If anyone had reason to turn in fury on the world it was she. Her gift to the world was the beautiful body of its Redeemer; the world's return to her was the gory remains of its orgy of hate. Yet she accepted that body without complaint. What was so obviously God's will was her will too. When in agony of soul she received His broken body from the cross she could no more take her anger out on the world than did Christ. When He was pleading with the Father for forgiveness for those who crucified Him, His prayer was also hers. The good nun can be identified by this same tremendous love. She could no more be deluded into thinking she loved Christ without forgiving her enemies than could His own Mother, or St. Stephen, or the countless martyrs who have died with the same pardon on their lips. When even those who have done the religious no injustice are the victims of her antagonism and spite, she surely shares very little with the Mother or the Son. The gross sins of libertines are less a scandal than the callous disregard of religious for their sisters, to say nothing of the relations of one community to another, or the relations between religious and the employees of their institutions.

The wonders of the Passion never cease. Jesus knew that He was going to die. He told the Apostles that He was going up to Jerusalem to do so. Yet He had not raised a finger to prepare a place for His burial. He simply was not interested.

There must be a deep meaning in this for the nun. He could not make His love for poverty more apparent. People mattered so much He died on the cross for them, but possessions were so unimportant that it was a matter of indifference to Him where they would lay His body.

Mary must have felt an urge to leave everything else behind and remain in the tomb with the sacred body of Her Son. But, despite her emotions, and who can doubt they were monumental, her consuming and single desire was to see the will of God perfectly fulfilled. Her Son had made it plain in His last moments that she was to be a mother to St. John and to the sons of men, even those who had crucified Him. Whatever may have been her feelings, whatever may have been her natural preferences, she was to be with the Apostles in their hour of need. She took one last look into the tomb and turned to find her Son again in His children, in His Church.

Modern religious need to do much rethinking in the light of this vocation of our Lady. Many would choose to bury themselves with Christ's remains in the tomb, leaving the world to its own devices. They lose sight of the Christ who said, "Let the dead bury the dead; come follow me." Admitted or not, religious have generally moved away in spirit from the people, as if to seek, uncontaminated, a high degree of union with Christ alone. Yet the cloister has no meaning without the people. All graces came through redemption and redemption was the gift of God to God for the people. Some have complained about or condemned the humanitarian emphasizing the brotherhood of man as if forgetting the fatherhood of God. But the religious themselves often promote the fatherhood of God while seeming to forget their brothers and sisters in Christ. The religious who actually does this has forgotten God. She is thinking primarily of herself.

And so Christ was, is, and must for all time remain the sole model for the religious. All that is positive in religious life she will find in Him. The rest remains negative and consists primarily in removing from her life, through realization of her weaknesses, mistakes, and errors, all that keeps her from being one with Christ, her Spouse for now and for eternity.

3. A Hundred Times as Much Now

GRACE is greater than the miracle which restores life to the body for grace gives supernatural life. It is the supermiracle. It does not give us the power to change our natures; it does enable us to change our ways. Christ does not expect His religious to change their natures, but He certainly does expect them to change their ways. Those who balk at this argue that human nature is being ignored or demands are being made which are unreasonable. St. Paul disposed of this subterfuge when he insisted that he could do all things in Him who strengthened him. What nun cannot be humbler, more honest, more generous, more thoughtful, more loving, more dedicated? Grace makes this progress possible and the love of God makes it necessary.

What follows here is not an effort to point out all that is wrong with religious and religious life. True, it is not an effort to congratulate them on the wonderful lives they are leading or the wonderful work they are doing. It is criticism. But it is criticism where there is room for it, of things not too well done, where error is to be found and mistakes corrected. The area of correction and improvement is the whole area in which the religious can increase her offering to God and beautify the gift she makes of her life. A gift is beautiful in the eyes of the giver only when she leaves noth-

25

ing more to be added. It is beautiful in the eyes of the receiver when He knows that it is all that she has to offer, the complete gift of herself.

The principle underlying religious life is the abandonment of all things for Christ: mother, father, home and lands, and ultimately oneself. For those so doing, Christ has promised a hundred times as much now, and later, eternal life. Christ, being God, makes no mistakes, utters no exaggerations. Therefore, if the one who gives up these things is not receiving a hundred times as much now, there is something wrong with the offering. It is not as complete as she thinks; it is not as sincerely made as it should be. She is withholding something.

How many religious actually feel they are getting a hundred times as much here and now? The answer, of course, depends on just how truly all things have been given up. Few who have really given up all things doubt that they have received the hundredfold and more. Few who know in their hearts they have not given up all things believe they have received it. They know full well that, although they have vowed their lives to God, in reality they have taken them back little by little under their own management and direction. This is the basic sin of the just: the lack of faith, the inability to take Christ at His word, to leave their happiness to Him.

The apparent simplicity involved in offering one's life to God is deceptive, however. The words come easily enough but the deed is another matter. The proportionate reward, a hundred times, should indicate that it is not as easy as it sounds. The fly in the ointment is that the hundred times goes to the one leaving all things behind her "for my name's sake." It is far easier to do this for her own sake than it is for the sake of God. The second of the sins of the just consists in the fact that the good person, despite all intentions to the contrary, seeks her own glory and satisfaction to a much greater degree than the glory of God. And although so prone to credit herself with the best of motives, when put to the test, she is usually capable of a higher degree of sacrifice for her own good name than she is for the name of Christ.

The young lady entering the convent wants something more than the world has to offer. "What doth it profit a man if he gain the whole world and suffer the loss of his soul" are very impressive words. Most of the things the world offers can be classified under prestige, power, or pleasure from position, wealth, or sex. The aspirant does not see anything in these to guarantee the enduring happiness she wants. Only union with God, real holiness, begun on earth, endures beyond the grave. Thus the novice is eager for holiness.

Her problem seems simple enough. Since giving one's life to God means holiness — and she does want to give her life to God — all she need do is continue on. Yet sadly, after several years of experience, or perhaps even after a few decades of religious life, the nun can wake up to the fact that she has little or nothing to show for those years. This is a startling discovery often leading to the cold, haunting fear that she has been living a lie. She has very little feeling for her life. The routine search for imperishable riches has apparently left her a pauper. She experiences a great temptation to panic, but this she must never do. She must force herself to relax while searching her soul honestly for the answer. It will not elude her for very long, although she may accept it only with great difficulty. Honesty has not been her forte. She believes that she has sought holiness, but can she see that from first to last it has been for her own glory rather than for the glory of God? God, loving her, and wishing only her salvation, will not let her be deceived. He left her on her own to show her that she could not possibly add a cubit to her own stature.

To the worldling, the prestige of position, wealth, and sex in some form means everything. She struggles for these things, expecting to find in one or a combination of them her full reward. Position makes her someone of consequence. Wealth buys her the things which make her the envy of her companions. Sex gives her a sense of being wanted, of having the power to allure. The preposterous thing is not that the worldling can want these things for her satisfaction but that the religious can reject them for the same reason, her satisfaction. For although the latter rejects them in favor of holiness of life, she does want holiness for her own satisfaction. The nun knows that most people lose the little happiness they had after getting money. She also knows that love seldom comes to those who covet it and never to those who demand it, that the fidelity demanded by true love cannot exist with gross selfishness. She appreciates too the bondage of being someone of consequence. But she does not see that holiness represents for her the same fulfillment so sought by worldlings from these other things, her satisfaction here and now.

It is precisely because the young girl has her heart set on holiness that she enters the convent; it is her holy grail. This being the common quest in the convents, each wishes to acquire it. But holiness, the goal of every religious, soon takes on a new dimension; it becomes an end in itself. It becomes THE mark of distinction in the convent since good people enter there with the weaknesses and foibles of their human nature.

The desire for holiness is not normally a bad thing. Thus restraint in the search for it seems unreasonable. But when it becomes the distinctive "Easter bonnet" of the cloister, it is certainly not sought solely for the glory of God. The same quality which makes a woman want to appear in an Easter hat more striking than her neighbor's can make one nun want to be holier than her sister. The same reasons which make a woman want to be wife of the president can inspire in the nun the desire to be the spouse of Christ. It is human to want to be someone special; the Apostles all wanted to be first in the kingdom. Holiness does make one special and it is all too human to want it for that reason more than any other. The aura of holiness gives a nun dignity and standing in the community. It takes a long time and many hard knocks to make the nun realize that it is not what happens within the cloister walls that matters but what happens in the heart. The walls do not effect as many changes in the heart as most nuns expect. The woman giving up her life for God only to possess Him as her proudest boast is missing the point. The glory of religious life is in being possessed by God — a fundamental distinction.

If the nun really wants the love of God, He will give it to her. However, when she wants it for her own glory, unconsciously or not, God simply cannot give it to her. It would be rewarding the servant who uses the master's goods for her own aggrandizement. In granting the prayer of the nun seeking holiness for her own sake God would be helping her to build a shrine to herself contrary to His clear pronouncement, "I am the Lord thy God and thou shalt not have strange gods before me."

Should she then ask for this gift which can be so easily misused? There is really little choice. She could ask for wisdom. But when Solomon asked it and received it with God's commendation, he still fell by the wayside. There may be many wise souls in hell but there are none there who love God. No, there is no better gift she could ask for, but it is not simply a matter of asking for it. It is for her, first of all, to know what she asks, and, second, to leave the accomplishment of it entirely in the hands of God. He not only knows what to do but how to do it. Coming from Him it will be true holiness, allowing her no delusions about herself. To ask sincerely for the love of God is to consent to the reduction of self-love. God never violates one's freedom to refuse His graces; thus her love for Him will depend first of all on her good will and then on her capacity for this love.

On entering a heart God immediately sets about increasing its capacity by emptying it of self. The soul can be filled with God only in the measure of its emptiness of self. The willingness to be emptied must not be merely oral but an actual desire to accept all that is involved in the process regardless of the pain and anguish. Her selfishness will be reduced to the very degree of her abandonment to God. Abandoned to God, her only disappointment is in the miserly degree of that abandonment. But the purification does not take place in a single experience. According to the threshold of pain, different in each person, she will cry out many times, "Enough, enough; I can stand no more." As God prepares to withdraw she perceives her mistake and humbly asks for His immediate return. Each time this happens she understands a little better what He is doing; she tries not to cry out again regardless of what He asks. When

He seems to ask a little more she learns to trust a little more.

The soul cannot clearly understand what God is doing. so she doubts the wisdom of what is happening. Yet, however dimly, she appreciates that if she knew the mind of God she would be as great as God. She learns to subject her plans to His arrangements; she leaves ways and means entirely in His hands. Hers is only the problem of the Apostles in the boat. They had seen His power and the strange things which had taken place at His command. Yet even with Him in the boat they could not conquer their fear of the frightening seas. It was plainly ridiculous to call His attention to their peril by rudely awakening Him. Still it is the fear of every soul, in the confusion of peril to self, that God has somehow or other lost sight of her. At this time she cannot be quite convinced that He is perfectly aware of the danger threatening her. Only when the seas are calm again does grace remind her that it was she who asked Him in the first place to undertake her sanctification; that what has happened was really only the answer to her very own prayer. It dawns on her with increasing clarity that He has left her to her own resources to let her see her hopelessness without Him. This is the story of every soul, for grace works no other way. It takes a long time to learn that all things will be accomplished in His time and in His way rather than in the way that she had planned. If she had learned it quickly without fear or bitter apprehension she would foolishly have taken credit for all that was accomplished.

As the nun advances in age and wisdom her self-esteem shrinks, not through depression or discouragement, but through her growing awareness of the great goodness of God. She begins to rejoice in her smallness, seeing it gratefully through the eyes of God as the condition for His gift to her. "Unless you become as little children," He said. The way is narrow, the road steep, and the gate small. Only children are not straitened in the narrow way, only they clamber up the steep paths, only they enter the small gates. As she decreases she still cries out at her diminishing size, but she knows that it is only her pride which is hurt; her chagrin comes from disappointment in self, not God. The humility which falls on her comes from measuring her dimensions against those of God insofar as they can be apprehended by the human mind.

Progress is assured the soul with the good will to let God make His plans for her, to see His plan in action in everything that comes along. That progress will be just as rapid as her humility will permit. Proportionate to her selflessness, governed by her honesty, her fearlessness and generosity will show how truly she lives her life for God.

4. The Truth Shall Make You Free

SINCE God is truth, union of the soul with God will depend on the degree to which the soul recognizes the truth and is willing to sacrifice all things for the truth. Love for God can be equated with love for the truth.

The great need in the nun's life is an all-pervading love of God. This must be a conviction of the mind. She must recognize it as basic truth. She will then place her life in God's hands, and the primary source of any ensuing confusion will undoubtedly be her lack of honesty. In view of this clearly understood fact it is staggering that religious can play with the truth for their own satisfaction when God has plainly designed the human intellect for the search for truth, for Him.

Anyone seeking God needs tremendous honesty, and it is very rare. It is difficult and at times it seems impossible to be honest. Despite the best intentions, fiercest desires, and most fervent prayers few have the bigness required for the virtue of honesty. Those insisting the loudest on their love for it will, with some objectivity, find they are deceived. For there is a world of difference between subjective and objective honesty. Whether the dishonesty is conscious or unconscious, it prevents the progress of the soul to God. Since He can neither deceive nor be deceived it is against

God's nature to build on a lie. Unless the nun sees things as they are rather than as she wishes them to be, God, by giving her the grace she seeks, would be building on error.

Genuine good will depends on honesty, a simple love for the truth regardless of how much it pleases or displeases her. But the virtuous medium of real honesty is very elusive. It is easier to presume that she is always right or to admit that she is always wrong than to develop the judgment to know when she is seeing the truth or only its facsimile.

The average religious may be slower to admit that she is wrong than is a worldly person. The latter is usually more practical: "The children of this world are wiser in their generation than the children of light." She knows what is materially good for her, here and now. The religious, intending only good, seldom doubts the goodness of her actions. Having invested her very life in religion, nothing could be more unpleasant than to see she is wrong in her approach to that life or her conduct of it. She is easily misled by wishful thinking. A man with large investments hates to think they are seriously threatened, but he knows that wishing will not safeguard them. The religious can too easily believe that if she blindly keeps on her way God will not permit her to fall into the pit. God gave her the eyes but she must open them.

Most people consider war a hateful thing. The innocent are killed, injustice is perpetrated, and useless destruction wrought. But people can be very detached from war if they are not to suffer serious personal inconvenience from it. Gasoline is rationed so they cannot travel as they please. Sugar rationing and the lack of bread or butter seriously inconvenience them. Some will not permit their fathers, husbands, brothers, or sons to die for any cause. Those who through birth control have not inconvenienced themselves to raise sons for their own defense don't feel the inconvenience of drafting the sons of others. While not a pleasant admission the real distaste of most people for war comes from their unwillingness to be personally inconvenienced by it. Religious, too, desire to live the good life and enjoy its blessings but not at the cost of being seriously inconvenienced.

The tests of honesty are daily and innumerable. How many hospital sisters feel conscience-bound to reprimand a nurse for being late for duty (often without inquiring into the cause) without feeling a comparable obligation to thank her for remaining overtime with a particularly sick patient? How many children are punished with a violence more proportionate to the teacher's indisposition than to the fault committed? How many nuns dutifully administer a correction in a manner they themselves would find quite unacceptable? How many consider the prime purpose of correction punitive rather than remedial? How often is the rule invoked to avoid some unpleasant chore, but conveniently forgotten to allow something enjoyable? How often do they come to the defense of their pets while remaining silent at the trials of those they dislike? How often does the religious exempt herself from any fault in injustice because it is not entirely her responsibility? How often does the guise of godliness cover her vindictiveness? But the dishonesty of the religious in relation to her work, her subjects, or her superiors is never the tragedy that is her dishonesty with God. It is not that the former is any less tragic, for dishonesty with neighbor is dishonesty with God, but direct dishonesty with God voids the very pledge she has made of her life to Him.

Much of this dishonesty originates in false teaching or misunderstanding of the truth. The former comes largely from inept teachers, the latter from overemphasis of one truth to the detriment of another. For example, the Church teaches that the sacraments give grace *ex opere operato*; from the sacrament itself comes grace if no obstacle is placed to it. To infer from this that the more frequently one goes to Holy Communion the better one becomes is quite misleading. It would be true, "all other things being equal," but in fact all other things are never equal. Thus many people who communicate less frequently are better than those who do so daily. Many religious wonder why, despite the fact that its members receive Communion daily, the community as a whole is not better than it is, and the members better than they are. Pastors by scores have wondered why so many of their troubles come from the "fervent" members of the parish; why the daily communicants can be among the most perverse, censorious, and selfrighteous. The distaste in the mouths of the less devout for religion, after association with the "elect," is proverbial. The fact is that, although the sacraments do give grace *ex opere operato*, the grace from them works in the soul *ex opere operantis*, or according to the dispositions of the one receiving them. That means they are fruitful according to the degree of love of God in the recipient. Frequence of reception does not in itself determine the progress of the soul in grace. This is the reason that preparation for Communion and thanksgiving after should take priority in religious life over less consequential devotions.

It has been made a virtue in religious life not to question the opinions of elders or superiors, even though Christ left Himself open to question by anyone. Every advance in science has come from the refusal to accept an axiom just because it is an axiom. Tradition is sacred but it is not infallible. If it were, Christopher Columbus would have died sitting on a dock in Genoa staring out into what was then considered space. Curiosity was given man by God so that he would seek knowledge through which he would learn more about even God Himself. However, religious have given curiosity a morbid connotation and built an aura of sin about it. The space age has taught us that we are only beginning a new era, and that the discoveries of the inquisitive mind are blessings for future generations. Exploration did not end when it was discovered that the earth actually was round.

One community after another has had its foundress canonized as if to prove that the rule handed down by her solved all problems for time and eternity. Yet the very opposite quality was the virtue of the foundresses. They went out and did jobs that traditionally had not been done and followers flocked to their leadership because they represented a ventilation of the staid and stuffy certainties. They established works which had not been undertaken and lived lives so unconventional that like Christ they were accused of being radical, misleading the people, and casting doubt on the untouchable *status quo*. The foundresses were the last to presume that theirs was the final word on anything. They were not like Hitler who wrote the constitution of the Third Reich to stand for a thousand years and shot himself so he could not see it dissolve in twelve.

Honesty is an unsettling thing. In others it makes one uncomfortable; in self it makes unpleasant duty much too clear. The main obstacle to it lies in the heart facing the inconvenience and trouble ensuing from it; it leaves no rest until one does what is right. The religious pledging her life to the God of truth cannot honestly believe in her sincerity when she does nothing about the faults she sees in herself. Perhaps that is why she prays with her eyes closed or is so concerned about the faults of others.

It is disturbing for a person to learn that the true picture of herself is not the one she has for years been painting in her mind. Honest people are not quick to accept compliments or slow to weigh criticism. When examining photographic proofs of themselves the normally dishonest people immediately enthuse about the flattering ones while considering the others not good likenesses. Yet the camera "sees" with mechanical precision, without respect of person. Perhaps it is oversimplification to say that one's honesty can be gauged by the willingness to accept an unflattering picture as one's likeness or to admit that a flattering picture is just that. Many nuns "honestly" deplore the seductions of Hollywood presenting everyone and everything in their most glamorous attire, and yet the community is turned inside out to find a novice beautiful enough to have her picture on its vocation propaganda, as if to create the illusion that most of the sisters in the community are or were once as pretty as the picture.

It is easier to wear a hair shirt than to face the truth. Perhaps this is the reason many women prefer penitential devices to facing the real issues. Honesty is the virtue by which the child sees that she deserved the spanking, the trollop admits that she brought her troubles on herself, the drunk confesses that no one else poured the whisky down his throat. Honesty is the virtue by which the religious sees that only she can stand in the way of God's work in her soul, by which she refuses to lay her failures at the door of persecution, misunderstanding, poor preparation for whatever happens, or any of the countless forms of self-justification. Honesty is the virtue with which she searches her soul for the obstacles to grace, wishing to find them regardless of their unpleasantness. The main stimulus to honesty is the prospect of its rewards which make the pain involved both acceptable and reasonable.

Honesty is the shortest route to union with truth, God. The goal is reached through the battle of the soul against slavery to self. The truth which makes men free liberates them from the emotional clamor for the immediate physical good, that which is seen, tasted, touched, heard, and smelled. It raises them above the senses where the prize of true love awaits the truly free. And there, for the honest religious, unenchanted by herself, there awaits the greatest love of all, the love of God.

5. Fearlessness

Love for truth demands great courage, for the truth reveals many unpleasant facts which will be faced only by the brave.

Courage is not easy to define. There are many pseudo virtues which pass for it. A very fine line separates the courageous act from the foolhardy one. In war a good man with a deep love for wife and family may show great fear in the face of the enemy. Yet a drunken philanderer, whose wife and children when out of sight are out of mind, may, after a night of carousing, rush an enemy post and wipe out a menacing machine-gun nest single-handed. Which is the coward and which the hero? While it appears that the former lacks the courage of the latter, it takes a great deal more courage to be virtuous than to be vicious. The first may have relied too much on himself or, being prudent, may have thought there were better ways to win the war than do it single-handed. The latter could have been an exhibitionist, the idea of dying in a blaze of glory appealing to him greatly in a moment of semidrunken exaltation.

It is hard to tell the difference between courage and exhibitionism in any given case, but it is not hard to understand that facing the truth takes more courage than the average man has. To build up courage one cannot just seek out occasions requiring it, like a medieval knight making a circuit of the joustings. But one can refuse to fear under any circumstances because God never takes His eye from one at any time, nor withholds the help required to be brave. The emotion of fear is salutary for man, and he must feel it always in the face of danger. But he can train himself to have the emotion of fear trigger the refusal to panic.

The nun entering religious life and undertaking the conquest of self needs courage. Since turning back is no answer, she must go ahead in the sure knowledge that she cannot be left to her own resources and that God never asks the impossible. Only panic can make her doubt this. "My grace is sufficient for thee" was the way St. Paul heard it. "God is faithful who will not suffer you to be tempted above that which you are able; but will make also with temptation issue, that you may be able to bear it" was the way St. Paul said it. The basis of courage is the sure knowledge that God gives help as it is required. Fearlessness is based solely on trust in God.

Fearlessness comes from practice. It comes from having gone into the valley of death and having come out alive; from having died to self and learned to live to God. It becomes more reasonable after every experience permitted by God to show a religious how truly He would be with her when she needed Him. On each occasion she felt that God had let her down and that her cry, "Lord save me lest I perish," had gone unanswered. Quickly she understood how wrong she was to doubt and on each occasion came closer to abandonment to God and complete trust in Him. Refusal to fear does not begin with the spiritual struggles in the soul. It begins with meeting the ordinary aches and pains of everyday life, refusing to compound them by anticipation, and comparing them without exaggeration to the great sufferings of the more seriously afflicted.

Self-inflicted pain is not the will of God. This pain is due mainly to preoccupation with self, and to anticipation.

In one hospital room there is a woman suffering from cancer. On the verge of leaving a loving husband and children she is inconsolable. She cannot understand why God visited this sickness on her when so many others were more deserving of the chastisement. She suffers mental anguish as well as physical pain in her rebellion against the inevitable. In another room there is a woman with precisely the same condition. She knows she has had a good life. God has blessed her with a good husband and wonderful children. She has every evidence of their love in the gifts they have brought her and the kindnesses she has received from them. She knows that she is the mother of her children but that God is the Father and will provide. This woman too suffers all the pains of cancer, but the pain is minimized by the joy in her heart, by her acceptance and her understanding that God could not wish her evil. Her pain is restricted to that coming directly from the afflicted organs and is accompanied by no self-pity or fear for self. Her one anxiety is to spare others unnecessary pain, to be brave.

Selfish people suffer most from fear. Anticipation of pain, while they are still physically comfortable, can bring sweat to their brows; any thought of suffering can make them tremble. The refusal to fear is quite beyond them as is the philosophy of suffering pain only when it really hurts.

Most people do not like going to the dentist — even though dentists have by finer technique, novocaine, and audio-anesthesia made the practice of their profession almost painless. But one person faces the inevitable and restricts the moments of pain to the dentist's chair. The other lets herself become the complete victim of anticipation of the pain. She is frightened when she phones the dentist for an appointment. She even hopes the phone will not be answered. When she receives her appointment it is the last thing she thinks of before sleep and the first thing on her mind in waking. She is no good the whole day of the appointment; she could no more read in the dentist's waiting room than she could enjoy a picnic on the way to the electric chair. She is delighted to see an office full of people ahead of her. When called by the nurse she can hardly get her feet under her. She feels nearly dead before she sits in the chair, yet she has suffered no actual pain at all. The nun who anticipates every difficulty along the road of religious life is like this. Most of the suffering she will never be called on to undergo; all the suffering she does undergo is necessary for her own good; none of it is wasted. Joy in life is all but impossible for her because she insists on making a five-act drama out of the least disappointment in life. Fortunately for such a nun God sometimes takes matters into His own hands. If then she is honest and refuses to fear for herself, her real life in God will begin.

This is what took place in the lives of the Apostles. Christ could have chosen men who would never have failed Him, but He did not. Whatever His reasons, they are consoling to so many who have so often failed Him. Christ did not choose dreamers, but practical, everyday people, catchers of fish, weighers of produce, collectors of taxes, hewers of wood, and tillers of soil. They gave up their livelihood to follow Him but they made sure He did not forget it. They were concerned about who would be the first in the kingdom and nothing He said about the beauties of purity of heart, meekness, poverty of spirit, or thirsting after justice lessened their intentions of inheriting the land. They wanted the kingdom here and now and intended to be alive to enjoy it. Palm Sunday was their first really encouraging day, their first glimpse of all they wanted to see and hear. The Pharisees had been put to shame, the tricky Scribes had been exposed, the money changers had been evicted from the house of God. At last the whole world was running after the Master, calling Him by the messianic title, Son of David, blessing Him for having come in the name of the Lord. This was sweet music to their ears; things were working their way.

The staggering denouement of the next few days all but killed them. Everything they wanted and longed for died. They were left speechless, heartless, lifeless. Christ in whom they had had such confidence had let them down because His ideas had not suited theirs. Even after three years of daily association with Him, watching His power, hearing His preaching, and listening to His descriptions of the kingdom, they still did not understand. Their plans for their lives were clear; they had no time for His. They set their own limits to what they would believe. They could not understand that which He had so often foretold, His Passion and death. And so at the very moment when Christ was doing more for them than at any other time, at the very moment He was dying to raise them up, the Apostles considered that He had let them down. So crushed were they by His death that they refused point-blank to believe in His resurrection, and told the women who brought news of it that they were crazy. They were the complete victims of their own fears. Then God took matters into His own hands. Christ came visibly to them and showed them their mistake. The coming of the Holy Ghost sealed their faith and made their trust in Christ indestructible.

This very thing happens in the lives of religious. They

must understand it as God's way of teaching fearlessness. The nuns love and esteem the state they enter. They have great plans for loving and serving God and anticipate the privilege of drinking His cup with Him — until it touches their lips and they taste its bitterness. It certainly is not the taste they expected. Such bitterness could not be from God. Then confusion enters, panic, and deep, cold, haunting fear that everything has been a terrible mistake from the beginning. Nothing is true, nothing good, nothing beautiful. The world outside and the heart inside are parts of the same great emptiness. Here is the beginning. Let the soul NOW refuse to fear. Courage is only the refusal to be victimized by the emotion of fear or deprived of union with God by anticipation of its demands.

6. Generosity

THE world gives endless testimony to the fertility of union. Man, sharing God's creative power, unites with a woman in love and their union is fruitful. But the greatest fruitfulness of all results from the union of the soul with God. The life of the soul immersed in God is marked with a singular generosity, deceptive only because it appears so effortless. The abundant fruitfulness of such a life is the indication that He who is mighty has done great things in the religious given without reserve to God.

The soul who knows that the love of God is all that matters is compelled to ask for that grace. Aware of its demands and knowing her own poverty, she trusts in God to the point of fearlessness. She finds her life unbelievably fruitful, without ever losing sight of the Source of her fecundity. Everything is testimony to the greatness of God. The most dangerous temptation of the good religious — the delusion of her own sanctity — is avoided, not so much by concluding that she does not have it as by never forgetting its source. In such a nun fearless abandonment to God begets tremendous generosity, the unstinting giving of herself.

It is not hard to distinguish false generosity from the real thing. The Gospel tells the story of the steward who bilked the master of much wealth but was successful in begging his acquittal. The same steward went out and all too humanly forgot what manner of man he was, throttled his fellow servant who owed him a pittance, selling him and his wife into slavery for the debt. Of course he received the reward of such action. He himself was sold into slavery with his wife and children until he had paid the last farthing. With the soul united to God, such behavior is impossible. Seeing the unbelievable generosity of the Master, she cannot rest until she does in like manner. There is never a time when she decides that she has done enough. She understands perfectly what our Lord meant when He said, "When you shall have done all these things, say, we are unprofitable servants." A life spent in giving would be for her only the least of beginnings.

For the soul reaching the heights of generosity there can be no shortcuts. There is no dispensation from the price to be paid. There remains only utter honesty, the terror of relying on God when help seems nowhere around, hoping through hopelessness. There is no way of purchasing holiness as Simon Magus thought to purchase the power of miracles. The fruit of sterile self-love is the pseudo generosity which brings tension, none of the easy abandon of the generosity born of the love of God in the secure knowledge of His inexhaustible largess. Tension identifies the nun practicing virtue on her own slim resources. Tension is the mark of the pseudo-virtuous, the self-conscious nun, the woman of fears. How can a religious actually living for Christ be so ever conscious of herself? Does a religious truly leaving all her cares in the hands of the Lord find great need of worldly comforts, the delicacies or luxuries that misguided parents or friends are sometimes so anxious to provide? Does the religious living real chastity find inordinate friendships so hard to abandon, or must she replace them by cold withdrawal from humanity as if she could be seduced by the love of neighbor commanded by Christ? Does she find obedience to a superior so impossible in view of Christ's obedience to Pilate? She does, if she is undertaking these things with her own resources, for her own glory, while demanding a disproportionate success. Wherever there is tension there is a religious working for herself; when she works for God she is relaxed and accomplishes greater things at less cost.

Inconvenience, want, friendlessness, injustice, and persecution are not beyond the acceptance of one who is convinced she has left the dung pile for the palace of a king. But they can and do break the spirit of the nun fashioning her own halo. They are the self-inflicted crosses of the religious casting herself in the leading role of her own epic extravaganza. Ananias and Sapphira could not resist the good company of the saints, but they would not go far enough to qualify themselves for membership. It is one of the more serious sins of the just that, insane as it seems, they insist on offering their lives to God while withholding from Him the complete use of them. If there is any reason for so many being called but so few chosen, it must be that the invitations have gone out but the wedding garments have not been put on. There has to be a withholding to prevent God's work in the soul. It is the chosen souls withholding nothing who enjoy the peace of Christ, the happiness of Christ, and the joy of Christ even amid the sufferings of Christ. It is an enigma of religious life that so many good people still insist on putting their own price on the priceless gifts of God.

7. *Objectivity*

OBJECTIVITY is the ability to see things as they really are. Subjectivity is seeing things through one's own eyes, or as one thinks or imagines them to be. Since all knowledge comes through the senses no one can be completely objective; a nun is objective to the degree that she does see things as they are.

Christ asked the blind man, "What wilt thou that I should do to thee?" To which the blind man replied, "Rabboni, that I may see." There is nothing the average religious needs more than to see. Her prayer to God should be, "Lord, that I may see." She should pray to see things as they are, not as she wishes them to be. The ability of the religious to be objective will determine to a large degree her progress in relation to God and to her neighbor.

So many things depend on the nun's objectivity that she must be careful to avoid the mistakes which reduce it. The sincere nun is convinced that things are as she sees them because she would not tell a lie. She must realize that her viewpoint is always biased in her own favor, by her own opinions and convictions. She must make allowance for this. Many also have been raised on the fallacy that the motive makes the deed; if they intend good they do good. But a mistake or an error remains an error whether intended or not. To insist that a right intention makes a right deed is to make competence and training superfluous. This fallacy has led to many tragic mistakes in religion, even to persecution carried out in the name of God.

It is not enough to want to be honest. People can be more observant, more alert, more interested. They can develop broader vision, more understanding, and better insight. But even people with great intelligence and integrity can be quite oblivious of a thing because they are absorbed at the time with something else. A music lover enthralled by a stereo recording of a masterpiece might not notice a gun going off next door. Yet he would willingly swear that such a thing did not take place because he was too near at the time to miss it. His oath to an untruth would have been honestly taken.

The Pharisees were so intent on their own ends that they identified their purposes with those of God. Through blind selfishness they were almost completely subjective about Christ. Because they saw Him as a threat to themselves, the leaders of the people, they saw Him as a threat to the Jewish religion and the Jewish people. They could thus "wisely" conclude that it was expedient for one man to die for the nation. Subjectivity made them discard His claims to Messiahship despite the undoubted signs He worked which proved His divinity.

Our Lord went out of His way to warn of subjectivity when He told the parable of the unjust servant who, forgiven much himself, throttled his fellow servant for a much smaller crime. His tragedy was that he saw everything from his own point of view. Had he not lost nearly all objectivity he would have been the first to see the enormity of what he did. Seeing things from his own little viewpoint he ultimately destroyed himself.

Objectivity is far more important to the religious than to others. The need of it is especially great among the cloistered orders. Living in the shrunken world of four monastic walls, unless the contemplative makes an heroic effort to be objective, small things take on unwarranted proportions for her. The mother general and her council can become the objects of an awe and respect not lavished on the president of the country and his cabinet. Lack of proper perspective can lead to mental illness or contribute to it in those already so disposed. The records show that there is a greater incidence of mental disorder among contemplatives than among the active orders where reality is not so readily escaped and objectivity is more easily maintained.

The religious has chosen the better part, and if she remains objective she will see that clearly. It is when she looks into a mirror and goes away presently forgetting what manner of woman she is that her trouble starts. Tied up in herself she complains that her Lord is long acoming and withdraws into herself. She becomes a neurotic, complaining self-pitier who loses all sense of privilege in being a nun. Despite God's predilection for her she feels her life bitter and unrewarding. She strains the gnat and swallows the camel, seeing everything from her little point of view. Given an assignment, she feels put upon and taken advantage of; if the appointment is given someone else she feels passed over regardless of her obvious talent and qualification for the job. She becomes one of the small religious shocking the laity by preoccupation with interior trivialities. The big sins of the nuns are not as shocking as the little ones. Religious are supposed to be big people who have given up the big things of life. They should be generous. When, therefore, smallness of mind and absorption in their own little worlds mark religious, they are a scandal.

The nun needs objectivity in her judgment of superiors. It helps her to see that if a superior is doing a 70 percent job she is a great woman. Granted that there is 30 percent wanting in her administration; any normal replacement would leave at least that much, though it does not appear so at first because the new broom always catches some things the old one missed. Objectivity helps a nun to see why former superiors look better and better. She is no longer bothered by them and their faults; she remembers their good points which are always better for being virtues the present superior does not have.

Two clichés betray subjectivity in the nun: the evasion of responsibility by saying, "That is none of my business," and the insistence that if she did bring a subject to the attention of authority, "It would not do any good anyway." One proves that her charity is all but dead; and the other, that her judgment is poor. A matter rests with authority only if brought there. To relieve oneself of the responsibility of bringing it to the attention of authority is to be derelict in duty. If authority chooses to ignore the matter — and certainly many small matters brought to the attention of authority through bad judgment or vindictiveness are better ignored — then the responsibility lies there. Too often authority is condemned for not taking action in a matter about which it knows nothing. Hardly objective judgment, to be sure. Such clichés make nuns indifferent and irresponsible. The woman dedicated to God shoulders, both in her community and private life, greater responsibilities than those she escapes by leaving the world. Since her burdens are greater she needs better and more objective judgment than the normal person.

Religious life has made its great advances under those religious superiors who have been most objective. Not only have the lives of their subjects shown the inspiration of a healthy approach to spiritual things, but the works of the order have flourished and the apostolate has been conducted with the joy expected of those with God in their hearts. Such superiors bring the best out of the sisters because they have expected a good performance of them and tried to develop their capabilities and talents. When they have given others responsibility they have not continued looking over their shoulders as if they could not be trusted or were incapable of acting with good sense.

The superior general who takes on herself every single decision of the community is not only being subjective, but she does the sisters a great disservice and injustice. Basically she may be abler and more intelligent than her local superiors but they know their areas better and are more familiar with the circumstances calling for decisions. If her decisions for their departments are made easily, they are usually irresponsible and bad. If they are made with difficulty she wears herself out needlessly at a job another, though less capable, can do better. Superiors general desperately need advice and the assistance of all available talent if they are to make wise decisions and plan successful programs for the community. Every nun should be trained to make and be responsible for decisions in her own sphere. She should be allowed to develop the good judgment to know when she exceeds her authority or falls short of using it. Only God makes no mistakes. The tendency of one tired old brain to do the thinking for a whole community of young and zealous women is a sure sign of lack of objectivity. Common sense of even a low order should make it plain that such a thing should not be done; that where it is done there is dreadful waste of energy and talent. This is an area in which an erroneous theory of the grace of office conflicts with common sense and plays havoc with the Mystical Body of Christ.

A superior needs objectivity when receiving the complaints of one sister about another, or reports of dereliction of duty. She has first of all to know her sisters and this she cannot do if she does not know herself. Some nuns cannot tell the difference between real evil and human weakness, between wrongdoing and the margin of error found in all human judgment. Superiors must be very objective to know whether their reactions to problems come from the wrong committed or from embarrassment at being called to account for the trouble. Superiors have to be objective if they are to be as zealous in guarding the sisters' liberties as they are in insisting on their obligations. They need it to treat their critics as fairly as they do their friends and admirers; not to let a trifle today become a tragedy tomorrow. When something goes wrong in the convent and the superior angrily asks why she was not informed of it, a courageous nun might say that it was because the last nun to report such a thing barely escaped execution for her trouble.

Superiors complain that the training of nuns in specialities often brings out the worst in them. Unable to stand the prosperity of education they become proud and unmanageable. More than one superior has said that she never had trouble with a sister until she sent her on for higher education. Such a superior is not objective enough to see in her words an indictment of the religious training rather than of the religious themselves, for surely the least religious training can do for a nun is prepare her to handle her own pride. Such subjective thinking won for the Church a reputation for keeping the people ignorant and poor that they might better save their souls.

The tragic effects of subjectivity are not restricted to religious and their lives. Much of history is a record of the slanted point of view of the historian which has led to unbelievable strife. Many "authentic" documents actually came from the pens of paid diarists recording the dictation of their patrons. Men had to eat and few *bona fide* historians were paid to be objective. Character assassination has marked the pages recording history and passed as the unvarnished truth from incontrovertible sources. Nor does it matter whether the motive was good or bad in writing these documents, the truth was tampered with and events were not recorded objectively. Even today with new methods and improved communications it is all but impossible to record contemporary history impartially. History has to be seen through the eyes of men whose prejudices are hard to escape.

This inability to be objective has been characteristic of the biographers of the saints as well as those of emperors and kings. It is difficult to discover the actual life of the saint in the biographer's record. The arbitrary selection of rumor and truth usually leaves the life of the saint at the biographer's mercy or at the mercy of his sources.

The *Autobiography* of the Little Flower is a striking illustration of the difficulties to be faced through subjectivity. Only lately did the public learn that the original document had been edited many times by her loving sisters, several thousand changes being made before it was released. One wonders whether one saw the Little Flower as she described herself or as the loving sisters thought she should be seen. Yet who would accuse the editors of bad intentions or designs?

The subjective treatment of the saints more than anything else has led to their portrayal as strange people who went about doing unusual things. This inclines the average person to feel dispensed from any serious obligation to imitate the saints, since they were not quite normal. Thus the religious when corrected can blurt out, "What do you expect me to be, a saint?" The reply of course must be "yes," for what religious really expects to be anything else? But lack of objectivity has made attainable holiness seem out of reach even to those vowed to the service of God. Little wonder then that religious get discouraged when they experience the middle-age spiritual doldrums.

Our Lord was objective. He deliberately chose His Apostles from the ordinary people to show that it was from these He would raise up saints. God was certainly objective in inspiring the Gospels, yet the evangelists did not cover up the betrayal of Judas, the denial of Peter, or the fact that Thomas doubted Him and the rest ran for their lives in His worst moments. Nor did they hide the fact that the Apostles were fighting among themselves about who would be first in the kingdom. Church historians writing today might prudently decide that these things were better omitted for the sake of the people.

There is tremendous need for objectivity in the apostolate. To see people as they are, to sort the facts from fiction, reality from rumor, to allow for the tendencies to judge others by oneself, and to color things according to prejudices, background, and experience, to be able to assay correctly the opinions of others, are all things which require an objectivity without which the apostolate is nearly useless.

So subjective are missionaries among pagans that they are surprised to find in them the same concepts contained in the Ten Commandments. These are generally considered to be Judaeo-Christian concepts rather than evidence of a conscience in every man. Missionaries sometimes foolishly think basic zeal and love for God are enough for their work. But when they are so "blinded" by their native prejudices that they fail to see, in the "ignorant" people they go to, cultures far surpassing their own, they commit the unforgivable discourtesy. Often the only real ignorance of these people is of Christ, which the missionary will never remedy if he loses their respect by being too subjective in his judgment. Identification of the blessings of Christianity with his own background and culture has led to his rejection by the very people for whom he has given up everything. Some missionaries could not even bring themselves to a thorough study of the language and customs of a people, as if expecting to be endowed with the gift of tongues or hoping that God would in some way communicate directly with them.

The subjectivity of the missionary is shown in his impassioned pleas for the help he needs to evangelize. He pictures non-Christians as longing for Christ, being deprived of Him only by the failure to provide a priest for them. Yet any objective listener would know that the people who had not heard of Christ could hardly long for something completely unknown to them. A little objectivity on the part of the missionary would enable him to explain just as passionately that he went to the missions not so much because those people wanted Christ as because Christ wanted those people. He would probably do much better in his collection too. The truth is always more impressive.

The object of religious life is union with God. It is all too human for the religious to seek a God who is a little like herself, but it is hardly being objective. Christ's crucifiers, while He was dying on the cross to win for them the grace of faith, were screaming at Him to come down and they would believe in Him. Those seeking God on their own terms should not be the least surprised if they never find Him. The religious who does not end up in His eternal embrace pays a horrible price for her willful blindness.

8. *Good Judgment and the Critical Sense*

TYRANNY is marked by intolerance of criticism. Where there is freedom there is criticism as surely as where there is sun there is warmth. The dictator alone insists that his people are happy; the people have nothing to say. Unfortunately there is too little room for criticism in religious life. It is generally unwelcome either because of the tyranny of authority or because of the poor judgment of the critics. In either case authority is not blameless. In the first instance it refuses what is good and helpful; in the second it has failed to develop the judgment of those who will perpetuate it. Religious have notoriously poor judgment as a rule, and perhaps because of rule. But good judgment is a basic need for anyone doing any good work, let alone for religious whose work is preparing the way for God's grace.

Good judgment is a combination of intelligence, objectivity, and the critical sense, enabling a person under normal conditions to make the right decisions for more fruitful living. It is developed by the use of the above faculties with reliance on the decisions made, to the point of normal prudence. It is an essential part of religious training to study, encourage, and develop the good judgment of the subjects, without which they cannot be happy, will not be responsible or productive, will lack the integration necessary for a full life in religion. The failure to do this has accounted for most of the neutral and negative personalities in religion.

Young people entering religion begin a new life. They have little to offer but their willing minds and attentive wills. But they are the riches entrusted to superiors in the name of God whose talents are to be invested in His behalf. God will demand five talents for five, and two for two. None are to be buried or left to lie dormant. Religious training must not reduce responsible young adults to the status of infants. They are not to be set playing spiritual "Ring-around-a-rosie," when the exercises can be much better orientated to their future state and its responsibilities. A young man is trained in a year or so to be a tough fighting marine ready to die for his country, while religious training can take six years to turn out spiritual cowards, judged unequal to living for God in a world demanding saints for leaders. That world is not impressed with second- and third-raters. It expects religious to believe in their own principles and to know why they do.

Training in good judgment can be given only by people who have good judgment, and these are very scarce. The system does not develop them. Religious with good judgment are so invaluable in many other positions in the community that they cannot be spared for training programs. And this is tragic, for while the system of training does not spoil those who have good judgment it does retard them. They are not encouraged or even allowed to use their own judgment. They are told to do what they are commanded without question, even though they are being told things by people without good judgment. Training in good judgment is given the way training in reading, writing, speaking, or pedagogy is given — there is the theory and then the practice. The students of good judgment have to be taught what is involved and then made to use it. Then they must be corrected and redirected and taught the proper degree of reliance on what they learn.

From the beginning of their training, religious must learn to make the required decisions. Many are a little contemptuous of the "decisions for Christ" stressed at evangelistic meetings of non-Catholics. But what else is a vocation? Too often the decision to enter religious life is the last one the religious ever makes, yet virtue is acquired under God's grace by good judgment and decision. Religious are called time and time again during their religious lives to higher spiritual living in deeper union with God. This call goes unanswered by those who lack the good judgment to see what it is and the decision to take the steps necessary to respond to it. The promise of virtue can be accurately estimated after a thorough study of the trainees. Who makes decisions precipitously tends to be rash and thoughtless. Who makes them slowly and fearfully tends to be timid and insecure. Successful decisions come from clarity of thought and vision, with an uncomplicating selflessness. Erroneous decisions come from pride, indifference, and undue preoccupation with self. The field of good judgment exposes the whole approach to the spiritual life, from the dark introverted halls of particular examen to the illuminated Thabors of mysticism. Many religious remain incapable of advancing even a little after years of examen while others sit deluded on a cloud of imaginary exaltation because they lack good judgment.

Whether it is because they are clothed in the godly garments of religion or because they forget that the best of them were made by God from nothing, religious are inordinately proud. There is no greater block to good judgment than pride. Based on a lie, on deception, pride makes an impossible site for truly constructive development. Whatever is built there has to crumble sooner or later. Pride causes religious to accept as axiomatic the principle that their weaknesses must never appear in public. They foolishly consider it is the appearance of weakness rather than the weakness itself which lets the Church down. Ostrichlike, they tend to deny the weaknesses which do not appear, and to withdraw from the world rather than come to grips with their pride. Nothing so fosters the delusion of perfection as deliberate blindness to flaws; nothing so leads to perfection as candid admission of them and purposeful dealing with them. The simplicity of this approach demands fundamentally good judgment.

Religious indicate bad judgment in several ways. They tend to let only the competent perform, forgetting that performance is part of training in competence. The basic obligation of parents is to develop the full potential of their children; the obligation of religious training is to see to the highest possible level of development in all its members. Religious tend to depend on the superior judgment of the few (which judgment is usually brought to the community, not developed in it), rather than strive for the highest degree of judgment for the greatest number. Good judgment cannot be developed where no one is permitted to question the judgment of those in authority.

It is the epitome of bad judgment to consider subjects disloyal because they see the faults of superiors and the failures of the community. It takes willful blindness not to see them. Intelligence, alertness, and loyalty to truth make it mandatory that religious see the flaws of their community and its works as well as their own. How else could their works for the glory of God increase in the intensity of their praise? The nun who demands support for her judgments without reference to their intrinsic merits, because the judgments are hers, does a disservice to God, the Church, and religious life in general. It is shocking to the world to see any religious superior or subject consider herself above question when Christ allowed Himself not only to be questioned but betrayed, denied, doubted, and crucified. Surely no religious could be so arrogant as to think she makes no mistakes. There is no better atonement for a mistake than admitting it, nor anything more disarming than a simple apology for bad judgment. It is a true sign of greatness in authority to permit anyone to question any judgment made. Authority never so successfully undermines itself as when it demands immunity from criticism or inquiry. Refusal to admit error in the face of evidence shows not only poverty of judgment but also poverty of virtue. The subject who does not allow a superior a margin for error is demanding that she be God. But when authority supports authority right or wrong, the standard of administration is reduced to the level of the superior with the poorest judgment. Divine Providence can only turn a deaf ear to pleas for miracles to do what common sense has already been ordained by Providence to accomplish.

No one's judgment is so bad that it cannot be improved; nor is anyone's so good that any help is superfluous. The wise man knows his own limitations; the fool discards with contempt the available help of better minds. The latter does not so much scoff at Christ as fail to notice Him at all. It is the duty of authority to demand the best from subjects. But the best minds err, and when subjects are dismissed or punished for being honest in error, they are rashly accused of revolting against God rather than of simply being human. It is the unfortunate responsibility of authority to make decisions, but no adviser should arrogantly demand that his advice be followed, for, although he does bear responsibility for the advice, he cannot be accountable for the use others fail to make of it.

Honesty is love for the truth; objectivity, the ability to see it for what it is. Good judgment is the ability to apply the truth for the good of one's soul and for the good of those for whom one is responsible in charity and justice. Like all virtues good judgment is acquired by practice. Zeal for the kingdom of God compels its exercise; prudence perfects it. It cannot be developed without risk of error. No nun is born with perfect judgment, nor can it be improved if never used.

There is only one sane reason for condemning criticism — the poor judgment of the critic. But even criticism must be heard before it can be condemned. Only the subjectivity of religious makes criticism unwelcome and causes them to treat it as an affront rather than the help it really is. Subjectivism confuses the loyalty of the critic to God with disloyalty to lesser authority; it blinds the lesser authority to her own affront to God. No religious intends to live a lie, yet she does so who knows she errs but refuses to admit it. Any religious intolerant of criticism acts this way.

It is strange that religious should consider the critic disloyal or uncharitable when he is highly paid for his opinion by the world. A good confessor is a critic highly esteemed by those who put a true value on their souls. The critical analyst of religious life would also be properly esteemed if religious were generally disposed to admit their mistakes and to profit by them. The quick resentment of criticism by the average religious and the alacrity with which she labels criticism negative and destructive indicates her blind love of self. Criticism has to be primarily destructive and negative if it is to be the basis of improvement. The performer of the arts wants to know what is wrong with his work so that he can correct it. The great artist has little time for comments on what he already does well. The whole field of progress lies in the area of poor performance. Compliments, while nicer to the ear than criticism, represent only testimony to what is already accomplished and are no real contribution. Religious should not be less interested in their performance than is the artist.

The religious loving truth learns a great deal from her reaction to criticism. She learns how subjective, oversensitive, and proud she is. If she dislikes her critics it is because they do not share her unstinting admiration for herself; their adverse opinions are unacceptable. Much of such a reaction is but emotional and to be expected, but when resentment continues and leads to real antagonism it challenges the honest soul to greater objectivity. It is possible to have such love of God and selflessness that criticism from any source is welcome. And with good judgment the criticism can be weighed for its inherent merit and usefulness. Discounting the normal, unpleasant emotional reflex to criticism and learning to weigh the critical opinion of others for its value involves the practice of many virtues. It offers a steady supply of mortification and contributes much to spiritual maturity. The ability to accept criticism graciously reveals a solidity not often found in people widely respected for their goodness.

The discerning person is astonished by the resentment of many good people toward criticism. They take everything so personally whether criticism involves their person, their theories, their religious community, or the Church itself. Despite their good reputations it is hard to credit them with much humility. The religious with the image of Christ before her, crowned with thorns, bruised and cut with reed and lash, should find it fairly easy to take any judgment passed on her. Certainly those contemplating the Holy Face should appreciate the luxury of being beaten with words alone.

Many houses are considered models of charity because criticism is absent. But in such a house there is apt to be more tyranny than charity in superiors and more indifference than charity in subjects. Charity is often erroneously allowed to cover everything from complete domination of the subjects by authority to such a lack of courage on the part of the subjects that they will not stand up for their own real good before God. In the first instance, authority usurps the place of God in the lives of the subjects; and in the second, the religious make intimidation for the kingdom of God's sake a virtue. Among the sins of the just are the presumption of the superior that she always operates for the best interests of the sisters regardless of her actions, and the assumption of the subjects that in the plan of Divine Providence they have no obligation to testify to truth. There is a world of difference between the stubborn religious confusing her own ways with virtue, listening to no advice whatever, and the calm, clear-minded religious willing to accept whatever censure is involved in doing what she believes is right. The former is a self-centered troublemaker; the latter is in the process of becoming a saint.

Sanctity is of course the goal of all religious, but no one can assume it will be attained without using the means available for reaching it. Intelligence is God's endowment for it, and good will is the offering of the religious. The use made of her endowment and all the good will she can muster will depend largely on her critical sense. If she is to reach the goal of sanctity, she needs this sense.

A major problem in developing the critical sense is the all too human desire to be right all the time, and the danger of letting wishful thinking make her believe she is. Nuns are good people wanting a good thing, and there is a tendency to think this is enough to assure obtaining it. Whether they are wrong by accident or design makes being wrong no better. Their fear of being wrong and its consequences can cause a withdrawal from making any decision when there is a real possibility of making a mistake. The more capable and qualified nuns are prone to indecision; the rash, to ambition. This very mentality which allows error to reign by default is the symptom of a sin of the just. Such a sin was the failure of the Apostles to share the burden of Christ's cross, and the failure of the beneficiaries of Christ's miracles to join Veronica in her mission of mercy. By the time they had faced their responsibility and recognized it as a privilege the occasion for it was gone.

Criticism is not to be eliminated, but given and accepted with charity. Authority is not to be used as a shield against it or docility as a dispensation from it. Superiors who learn to give it graciously and subjects who learn to give it respectfully both bear witness that their common interest is God.

9. Emotion and Reason

MAN's glory is his intelligence. He can think. There are few problems he will face which cannot, with God's grace, be solved by thinking them through. He will not always be right, of course, but he need only follow the best judgment he has and be willing, when he learns that he is wrong, to make the necessary adjustments. One of the deadliest obstacles to clear thinking is the tendency of the emotions to usurp the place and work of the intellect. This is work that the emotions simply are not qualified to do, and it should be no surprise that the results are disastrous, even catastrophic. The prevalence of this tendency is revealed by the number of people who say, "I feel that . . . " when in reality they mean, "I think that. . . ."

Many times a nun can be sure she is thinking when any impartial observer could see that the answer was arrived at with little or no reasoning. This is not only the case with the obviously emotional nun, it is more or less the case with every nun, many of them intellectually able, academically trained, and highly qualified. Much emotional predominance comes from the personality of the individual and her environmental background, but a great deal of it comes also from the failure in religious training to make a thorough study of the emotions. Such a study would enable the reli·

gious to recognize when the emotions are at work, and help her to go about her business making right judgments and performing right actions despite her emotions. A very emotional person can have a high degree of efficiency while working under emotional stress if she understands the emotions and disciplines herself to reasoned purpose. When understood the emotions are great indicators of the proper course to be taken. When not understood they create confusion, inability to cope, and a general sense of hopelessness. Many a nun says, "I know it is my emotions which upset me but that doesn't help. I still have very strong feelings and terrible guilt. I still have overwhelming and distressing reactions."

Recognition of the emotions does not eliminate them. Will power must be used in refusing to be *upset* by them. This is not done by fighting or resisting them, but by recognizing their work and ignoring them. A good helmsman does not abandon the boat to the forces of rough water but steers a course through them. If emotions are understood and accepted as part of the human picture and then limited to their proper sphere of action, their persistence, violent or subtle, will seldom cause a real upset. Their control, of course, is characteristic of the stable, mature person. Understanding and control of them is nowhere more important in the life of the nun than in the realm of purity or sex, for there, due to false notions, improper instruction, or lack of instruction, she is very apt to demand of herself the reactions of an angel rather than a human. This will be discussed further in the chapter on chastity, but in almost every phase of her life chaos or calm will prevail according to her emotional control.

Because so much distress can be traced to the emotions, they must not therefore be considered evil. They are part of human nature and as such reflect the glory of God as much as any other endowment. They have their very excellent purpose. The fact that man has not learned to understand and handle them properly is the source of the trouble. They are of great value in the spiritual life; the human soul has need of the assistance they can render, in much the same way the intellect has need of the senses through which all knowledge comes. Without the emotions, the avoidance of serious sin would be all but impossible. Yet because sin so often involves the emotions they are apt to get the blame which can only be truly placed on the intellect and will. One often hears the statement, "Her feelings just carried her away," as if that were a completely reasonable excuse for wrongdoing. In reality her feelings are far more apt to contribute to her virtue than her vice if she controls them instead of becoming their victim.

As a faculty of the spiritual soul the intellect has no feelings. Feelings are inextricably interwoven with flesh and blood. When a problem is presented to the intelligence it works it out step by step. The answer is passed on to the will for execution. According as the emotions are not allowed beyond their proper sphere of influence, and the will is disciplined to right doing, the work of the intelligence is rendered more efficacious.

The emotions are very different from the intellect. They are faculties of the body not the soul. They are shared with the brute animals which can become quite upset when taken out of their proper environment and spoiled by domestication. The emotions are called feelings for the simple reason that they are felt like a pinch or a nudge. They give an awareness of something to be dealt with or considered. A man may be absorbed in a book while something which would normally interest him intensely is passing unnoticed. A companion nudges him, calling attention to this occurrence which he would otherwise have missed. The emotions are the nudgers, the pinchers, the body calling the attention of the mind to something it should know or deal with. The emotion of love points out the lovable, attractive person; the emotion of hate, the threatening enemy; fear, the impending danger; pity, the compelling charity; and so on.

Doctors call sickness psychosomatic in which the emotions are involved with real physical ills. The man with ulcers has anxiety from unhappiness in his home or at his work which stimulates a secretion damaging his stomach. Asthma is largely due to psychological factors as are many skin eruptions and other things which were hitherto considered infectious. Doctors know that man's mind and his body have profound effect on each other. But since one is pure spirit and the other pure matter, they do not know where the connection is or just how it is made.

While scientific probing has opened so many of nature's other secrets, the doctors still don't know this one although they are more interested than ever in the answer. Suffice it to say that when they do learn it, the emotions will be highly involved because they do command the attention of man's mind through his body. They are contact-makers between matter and the mind. They could well be called the triggers of the intellect. Unfortunately when they are not understood and used they are apt to take control. There is a great difference between a friendly nudge from a beloved companion calling attention to a sunset to be shared and the hot breath of a black bear encountered on a dark night camping in the woods. The one nudge puts the mind into gear to consider the glories of creation; the other, when it does not completely paralyze, puts the feet in gear to take flight.

The emotions are very useful. They act like amber traffic lights. These lights are not meant as a threat but as a safeguard to life, making a certain amount of time available for the thought and action required to meet the situation they reveal. Yet many nuns look upon the emotions as occasions of sin, or as things to be put away and forgotten if that is possible.

Suppose a nun is teaching school. One of her misbehaving charges attracts her attention. Following the golden rule of pedagogy, she notices only half of what she sees. But the troublemaker oversteps himself, making it impossible to ignore the situation. The nun feels anger rising. Unfortunately she considers herself to be actually angry whereas she is only emotionally upset. The emotion of anger alerts her to the fact that she is heading for the sin of anger if she does not check herself in time. She has committed no sin; in fact she is in no real or imminent danger of committing sin. She is being given enough time by the warning grace of her emotion to get the situation within herself under control. She has time to say, "If I am not careful I will become quite angry with this boy." She immediately uses her ingenuity to master the situation and avoid the sin of anger. All the emotions help similarly in the practice of virtue. There would be very little virtue if the emotions did not alert one to the opportunities for its practice. Driving a car would indeed be hazardous if traffic lights went immediately from red to green. The amber light or the interval between lights gives ample time to take the necessary steps to cope with the change of traffic.

There is a reason why nuns rely less on their emotional warnings than the ordinary person. The convent rule makes them to some degree superfluous. Just as the rule of silence makes the amenities of polite speech for the most part unobservable, so do the highly controlled recreations and customs drastically reduce the occasions when nuns would find the warnings of their emotions helpful in meeting a specific trial. People in the world have to meet and do business with many others they do not like. To do this successfully they have to rely heavily on their emotions. The distaste they have for a person sets up a reaction warning them to handle the situation with caution if they hope to benefit from the contact. When the alarm is given, the intelligence presents the right procedure and the will commands its execution.

The same emotional control which makes it possible for people to get along together makes the practice of Christian charity possible in human intercourse. A nun will say she cannot help her emotional reaction to another nun. That is true because the emotions are given to render a true report rather than to deceive. But what the nun intends to express is the very opposite of what she says. She implies that since she cannot help her emotional reaction she cannot help her personal reaction and this is far from the truth. As a mature adult she should be in command of herself and, through proper discipline, she certainly can control her personal reactions. This is what Christian charity means. It is acting in a way pleasing to Christ, in conformity with His teachings, when her emotional inclination would be to the contrary. Her normal reaction tells her plainly what her emotional inclination is and gives her time to handle it.

Convent rule takes care of so many situations in which control is normally exercised that it precludes much of the practice of the virtues required by such occasions. Thus, for example, religious sometimes lack real courtesy. Certainly there is little occasion for it in convent life. With silence and solitude and the activities of other times so closely regulated there is little scope for courtesy. Customs determine who sits where, or who goes through which door first or into what pew. There is a natural penalty for this, so religious have to make greater effort to be thoughtful and courteous than people in the world.

Visualize what a woman's life would be without her emotions. With no emotional warning, anger would be upon her immediately. With no sexual emotions she would be in as much danger with one person as with another for she would have no indication as to who or what circumstances could be an occasion of sin for her. Without emotions she would have precious little notion as to whom she should marry, or with whom she could have the required rapport for a good marriage. What would listening to beautiful music amount to if there were no emotional reaction? What thrill from a magnificent sunset in the country? The sight of grief could excite no pity nor could tragedy evoke compassion. This does happen to some people. It is a shocking thing to see a person with no emotional reactions. There have been people who have suffered such extremes that they are no longer capable of emotion. Some of the victims of concentration camps were like that. They could see the most heinous crimes take place without reaction. They were reduced to a subhuman level from living in circumstances where the limits of human endurance had been passed. If religious life were calculated to do such a thing it would be a gross insult to the Creator. In relation to the emotions religious life is to control not obliterate them. Not every occasion of emotional challenge is to be removed from religious life, as some would have it. Such a plan could never develop emotional control just because it removes all occasion for practicing it.

The real calamity for the religious occurs when she is so upset by her emotions that she fails to see the hand of God in her life. She looks upon herself as a failure because she cannot rise above her emotions; or worse, she considers religion to be a fraud because her emotions do not cease to function when she enters it. Having asked God for the grace to love Him with her whole heart, her prayer is answered. Suddenly, for no apparent reason, she finds that she is misunderstood. She is stunned because she has been as sincere with her superiors as she has been with God. She hears things said which hurt her terribly. She feels badly treated, emotionally crushed. Seeing injustice in this she cannot believe that it is the work of God. She is confused and does not understand that while God does not deal in injustice He does make use of it to accomplish His ends. The nun who so gladly willed to be decreased is now so emotionally upset by the acts which cut her down to size that she is blinded. She *feels* that all is lost, that she is persecuted; she has little taste for her life in religion. If she could only be objective and unemotional she would understand that her love for God could never be purified so completely as when it comes purely from the will.

What she would like to see, of course, is that God is making her into a very holy woman. That would so delight her that she would not be long in thanking God that she is not like the rest of the nuns in her community. To love God truly and not herself she must go through a period in which she sees herself as she is, her spiritual poverty, uselessness, complete dependence on God for every last thing. This period must be long enough and emotionally distressing enough so that she will never forget it. All knowledge coming through the senses, the spiritual experiences not accompanied by acute suffering for an appreciable period are generally forgotten. What the religious learns herself she will soon forget, but the lessons God teaches her will never be forgotten. Because the nun feels hurt, dejected, and depressed she is ready to quit. This is strictly an emotional matter. If she learns to control her feelings and to look under the things that happen for the graces God has hidden there, she will value these experiences for what they are, very precious lessons in the way of love. This power comes only with time and trial. It is a hard thing to let consolations or distress come and go as God sees fit but it is the pattern of holiness. Nothing convinces one of the folly of emotion in religion as living among emotionally religious people. They go to church and sing and shout as their emotions direct. Yet when they have no feeling for it they could no more go to church than they could swallow bitter medicine if they were not sick.

Some religious go through great emotional upheavals when they are moved from a parish which they like, where they worked with a pastor who appreciated their help and valued them as friends sharing his life and labors. Their clamor would lead one to think God was burning them at the stake, even though while things suited them they were forever insisting that they lived for God alone. Religious professing detachment speak of *my* convent, *my* mission, *my* school, *my* floor in the hospital, *my* whatever-it-may-be, without any sense of impropriety. Certainly no one is supposed to feel elated at leaving places and people she likes, but surely an adult religious should be able to understand that the conflict is purely emotional. Wishing to love God and serve Him faithfully, she should consider occasions of emotional rebellion as golden opportunities to offer something worthwhile to the One who offered Himself for her. She should know that the emotions are not instruments of torture but signposts to sanctity. Few indeed negotiate the journey to holiness without their guidance.

When minor matters take on the proportions of major calamities the emotions are surely out of control. They have usurped the place of reason and one is being guided by a pilot with no competence. Like children quick to take the measure of the teacher, the emotions have taken advantage of the license granted them and no sense will be made of any situation until they are back in their place again. The will must police them. The intellect has sinned in permitting the emotions to do its work. Just as charity is not charity when one religious for her own satisfaction has relieved another of her responsibilities, so the religious who dispenses her intellect from the work for which it was given her does badly. She is unstable and her superiors must recognize it.

It does seem at times in religious life to be a virtue not to think. Many religious feel that they get along better if, like dumb beasts, they simply accept the dictums of those directly in authority. This is dereliction of duty and a failure in the fundamental purpose of religious life. Permitting oneself to be "brainwashed" before rendering the offering of oneself to God is like presenting God an empty box. God dwells in people, not in boxes, and the person whose mind is as good as new because it has never been used is an empty box, a shell, the travesty of a human being. The nun entering the convent to escape responsibility, fearing that the use of her intelligence can only make things more difficult for her, has a negative and unhappy life ahead. Most nuns know this; but there is trouble when the situation is not clear. When a nun has made a good generous start in religious life and the consequences of using all she has for God become too much for her to bear, if she contents herself with becoming a mere automaton she defrauds God. The sin is not so much that of Ananias, withholding from God, but rather of seeking her own comfort after embracing a life supposedly for God.

Unused intelligence is like the buried talent. The nun who realizes that she can never possibly do enough for God is delighted with her talents for they afford her the opportunity of making some return to God. It is the selfish nun who feels no remorse at wasted talent. She treats it as if it were not there because she does not want to see it, and she even makes a virtue of denying the existence of her gifts. The talented, of course, must not let their emotions dictate a pace suited to their fervent desires rather than their reasonable limitations. The person who lets misguided zeal run away with her reason is as culpable as the lazy, indifferent soul who entered in the first place because there was a depression, work was scarce, the rent was due, and anyway she was tired.

Certainly it is difficult to go through life using the intelligence. But since it is God-given for a purpose, that purpose cannot be spurned. Those who do this can justify themselves only by a false humility which is basically pure emotionalism. There are the religious who demand that no subject have higher standards than themselves. They are like the drunk whose only satisfaction in life comes from meeting a drunk worse than himself. They are insecure. The Pharisees would have been quite content to let our Lord go His way if they could have found some weakness in Him.

However, since they could not, and since His words and works made them look so bad, they had to change their ways or get rid of Him. Little men who have not grown can only appear big by cutting down the giants. This may appear to be progress but it really isn't. There is no replacement for the light of reason, not even the light of faith. One may not serve God by the use she makes of her reason, but she cannot serve God by refusing to use it.

10. The Grace of Office

THE grace of office is that by which the superior is "led" to give the family of the Lord its measure of wheat in due season, thus pleasing Him exceedingly. It is the grace given superiors to fulfill their responsibilities and duties to the highest degree of their ability. Grace is a personal thing and it is given the superior for the superior. It is not given the superior for the subjects, although the subjects of any superior making use of even a small portion of the grace she receives will profit much from it indirectly. It is a grace given the superior for the job she has to do, to be what she ought to be so she will do what she ought to do. It does not do the job for her.

The general understanding of the grace of office is very sketchy. There are many strange notions of what it is. The grace of office is not a thing which takes a woman of small mind and limited capacities and suddenly endows her with talents and qualities she did not have before taking office. The grace of office does not bless the errors of a superior and make them right. The grace of office does not take a person lacking understanding and stability and suddenly make her a haven of charity and a pillar of confidence for the afflicted subject. The grace of office does not place a superior's actions above criticism or identify her decisions with the will of God.

The grace of office does not give special enlightenment to a superior to pass unerring judgment on the thoughts, words, and deeds of her subjects, or to justly dispense rewards and punishments in the name of God, or to licitly deprive them of their rights and privileges under natural, divine, and ecclesiastical law. The grace of office does not superimpose all the required qualities of a good superior on the one elected or appointed to an office. It would be wonderful if it did, for the Church and religious life would certainly be in better condition than they are.

Just as nuns are not endowed with holiness on entering a community, superiors are not endowed with special talents or virtues on taking office. However, just as truly as religious do receive the grace to aspire to and acquire holiness, so too do superiors receive the grace to aspire to and acquire the qualities needed for a good performance of their duty, although few superiors see that one of the ways to acquire these qualities is to make the use they freely have of the good qualities available to them in their subjects. To make good use of the grace of office, the candidate must be honest enough to see and admit her shortcomings, to have the interests of God, the Church, and her subjects so much at heart that she will make any sacrifice to do a better job. This takes such humble discernment and unselfishness that few superiors are ready for it. Their new position and authority do not help them to see themselves as they are, although it is now doubly necessary to do so.

Authority comes from God, the authority of parents over their children as well as the authority of religious superiors. Parents must administer their authority in a way worthy of its source and for the good of the children. The term "father" is meaningless apart from the Fatherhood of God. When

Christ said, "Call no man your father," He was not denying parents the use of this title so much as pointing out the total paternity of God. All other paternity, whether pro-creative or spiritual, is such only in the restricted sense of paternity under God. When authority is exercised by parents in a manner unworthy of God, the obligation of children to obey ceases. No parent can forbid a child to enter religion and the service of God. So it is with the authority of religious superiors. They act beyond their authority when there is conflict between their commands and the laws of charity. The superior who demands a loyalty to her con-flicting with loyalty to God commands the impossible, nor can a superior command anything conflicting with the rules and constitutions of the order, or with loyalty to the superior general. No superior has authority greater than the power she represents.

Needless to say, the Church always upholds authority for the simple reason that it does come from God. It is assumed, until there is sufficient proof to the contrary, that the person in authority acts properly. But there is often reason to conclude otherwise and the reason must be heard or serious injustice unworthy of God will be perpetrated in His name. Error can never be upheld in the name of God. If religious are supposed to have the humility to admit their mistakes, superiors can be expected to have greater humility and double the reason to admit their errors. Their failure to have this humility and give the proper example is the scandal of authority abused. It underlies all anticlericalism and schism. Of course, as long as the authority of God is administered by human beings there will be honest error, which is no less error for the fact that it is honest. The greatest tribute from subject to superior is the acknowledgment of her ability to see and admit her mistakes and to apologize to her subjects when injustice has been done. Such a woman is superior in every way; her authority is seldom used other than for the glory of God and the good of souls. She dissolves criticism by hearing it and wins her critics by generous espousal of their just causes.

Communism is condemned because it insists that the individual exists for the good of the State. When the superior forgets that the order exists for the good of the individual, God is badly served. The doctrine of private interpretation of Scripture has been equally condemned. Education would be a waste of time if the Holy Spirit informed each man of the meaning of Holy Writ regardless of his intellectual capacity for learning. Yet there are those who infer from the doctrine of the grace of office that authority enables an ignorant, self-seeking superior to produce feats of genius and generosity normally beyond her. Some believe that the grace a superior receives not only endows her with an ability she does not have, but even protects her from her own folly. Such a concept insultingly attributes to the Holy Spirit deeds completely unworthy of Him. The Sanctifier is much maligned by these servants who make use of Him. How many elections of major superiors are attributed directly to Him rather than to the simple permissive will of God? Many a religious of edifying simplicity admits she is incapable of fulfilling high office, only through some strange quirk of fate to become a superior general.

At a general chapter enough electors, unwilling, perhaps unconsciously so, to support a more able and purposeful person, elect a compromise candidate because she was considered no threat to the status quo. She is truly stunned by this event. Apparently picked out of thin air, more surprised than anyone, she is the first to attribute her election to the Holy Spirit. Since she did not aspire to the office or have the slightest suspicion that she would be elected, her naïveté blinds her to the venality of the electors which, rather than the intervention of the Holy Spirit, brought her to power. She assumes her office amid tears of unworthiness on her part and tears of edification on the part of others. She will be a very great woman indeed if she does not soon consider herself to have the devoted guidance of the Holy Spirit and value His direct help more than the advice of the councilors elected to compensate for her known deficiencies. In acquiring the qualities and help needed for her job she is most handicapped because she is convinced that she was "chosen" especially for it. She conceives of herself as a sort of John the Baptist, making plain the way of the Lord. She goes ahead with her plans with an ever increasing sense of divine approbation, brooking no interference. Who questions her wisdom doubts God. She lets nothing stop her, reason, the advice of competent people, or even the "accidents" of Divine Providence. She has an eerie penchant for convincing some sterling souls of her mission and casting doubts on the wisdom of her equally elected advisers. Pointing out that the constitutions do not oblige her to follow their advice, she forgets that reason does oblige her to listen to it, to ponder it.

No superior as no subject can be obliged to go against right reason, but every superior as every subject must have reasonable assurance that her reasoning is right. Nor should she fail to see the tendency to consider it right because it is hers. The heretofore unworthy one, convinced of her election by the Holy Spirit, finds a strange reliance on the talent she admittedly did not have, and confidently draws on a wisdom largely nonexistent. This phantom wisdom is responsible for many of her selections of local superiors, which by experienced administrators would be attributed more correctly to her admiration for those who agree with her. Here of course enters the villain, politics.

To many, because of the prevalence of corruption in it, or more correctly because of the publicity given corruption in it, the very word "politics" is odious. Yet no organization can function without politics. The finest, most detached administrator in the world, trying to do the best job she can for God and man, must rely on others. In seeking qualified people to help her she can only search among the people she knows, or people known by those whose judgment she trusts. Very often the best qualified people are not among these and so do not come to the fore. But how else can an administration work? Certainly wise superiors never cease searching the ranks for competent personnel, but the grace of office does not supply a wisdom that is not there, and it does take wisdom to do this.

Unfortunately, too many religious are unwilling to take a leaf from the book of commerce and industry, "because religious life is not a business." But it is a business in the sense of being an organization of people for a cause. Industry spares no effort or expense to acquire suitable personnel for the responsibilities involved in successful enterprise. Perhaps Christ recommended this leaf when He praised the children of this world for being wiser in their generation than the children of light. It does seem that the moneymakers of the world are more anxious for their interests than are those working for Christ and souls.

Even in commerce the supply of adequate personnel is not sufficient for the promoters. Nor is it in religion. There just is not an adequate supply of superiors, or, better, a supply of adequate superiors. Some of this can rightly be attributed to the failure of those in power to train their successors, but much of it can be traced to human failings, and to the fact that the large majority of human beings must be directed by the few regardless of the prevailing system. The superior general and her council have no trouble filling some of the important positions. There are always highly competent people who can fit equally well in most positions. But the rest of the jobs have to be filled with the people left, from those who have some shortcomings to those who are all but complete misfits. They say that it is the dream of every basketball coach to meet a nice girl with a brother seven feet tall. It certainly is the prayer of every superior general that she will find more competent people around her than she can use. But the superior of even a little wisdom knows that with most appointments must go the hope, the harried, prayerful hope, that the appointee will be a success. The real sin of superiors does not consist in the appointment of those they know to positions of authority, but in the all too common human weakness of considering those who agree with them and their policies as the best selections. This weakness of the right is balanced by matching weakness of the left, the rejection of dedicated people because they disagree with their policies and opinions, without hearing them or weighing what they have to say for its objective value.

Superiors honestly interested in acquiring the qualities needed for their work must avoid two things. They must not be or permit their subjects to be deluded with the idea that superiors are smarter or more effective just because they are superiors. If a woman did not have the makings of a good superior yesterday she does not have them by reason of her appointment today. This delusion forces its victims to consider it arrogant pride on the part of subjects to doubt the greater endowments of their superiors when common sense would tell any dispassionate thinker the right answer. Second, superiors must never feel the necessity of covering up their defects for the sake of the Church or the order. It is not necessary to publish them in the local newspaper, but surely they let the Church or order down more by denying them than by admitting them. Their time is needed for overcoming, not camouflaging, them. How can a worthwhile subject expect reasonable guidance from a superior almost totally blind to her own faults? It is sheer folly to expect the average subject to take correction when the superior who should be the first to give example turns livid with rage at the slightest affront. Nuns who are teaching the people that parents are the first teachers and must give good example in their homes can go back to their convents as superiors and forget that they must be the first to give example in the convent. Being a superior does not provide an automatic dispensation from all the rules and regulations, least of all the urgency to holiness.

The grace of office has been misunderstood primarily because of the tendency of weak human beings to cover their shortcomings with the dignity of their office and to consider any personal affront an attack on authority and God. This is totally unjustifiable. It is more reprehensible in religion because religious life is dedicated to love of the truth, practice of virtue, and overcoming human frailty. It is pitiful and disappointing to see greater vanity and arrogance in religious authority, reputedly scorning the vanities of the world, than among the laity in the world.

The grace of office is that needed by a superior to fulfill her duty as a superior, to do her job. It doesn't make her something she is not, but, like all grace, "leads" the one open to it to "see" the big picture, what she must be, and the wide field of what must be done to be a good superior. It moves her to undertake her work, first of all within herself.

What is her work? She is a superior for only one reason, the good of her subjects, their welfare. Her first obligation is to lead the way in virtue; not to be the holiest, but to place no obstacles in the way of God in her life, and to do everything to make sure God comes first in the lives of her subjects. She does this mainly by demanding of herself what by virtue of her office she expects and hopes for from her subjects. She must learn that she cannot command respect from them; she must inspire it. She must understand that she cannot take away their liberty; she must teach them how to use it. Like a mother, she must expect sometimes to fail, regardless of all the effort and good will in the world, simply because her children have been given minds and wills of their own. She will have to make herself understand that freedom was really God's idea in the first place; to arbitrarily restrict it is to cast doubt on the wisdom of God. Arbitrary restriction of the liberty of the children of God, unreasonable insistence that "mother knows best," drives many children from home into rebellion and tragedy. How wise one has to be to know how to handle one's own liberty, let alone the liberty of others!

There is no heartbreak for a mother like seeing her child go astray. She is powerless to save her. Many thoughtful religious are grateful to God for not having to watch their own blood children turn their backs on home and God.

But the real mother does not rant and rave and curse the fruit of her own womb. Her sorrow is lost in pity for her child. Only the selfish mother can place her own hurt pride above the damage the child does herself. Understanding and forgiving sorrow is the message of our Lord in the incomparable story of the prodigal son. Any outrage felt by superiors in the failings of their subjects comes from their proud embarrassment, not from the affront of a sinner to God. They love neither God nor subjects so much as themselves.

But a mother can also fail her children by overprotectiveness, by preparing them too solicitously against dangers rather than to meet the dangers which are a part of everyone's life. A mother's proper provision for her children must be positive rather than negative. Superiors tend to think they have done all possible for their subjects when they have protected them from every imaginable occasion of sin, but they must rather provide the best possible opportunities for their personal holiness. Faulty training places far too much emphasis on occasions of sin and far too little on occasions of virtue. Religious cannot afford to be trained cowards. There are certain dangers which they must face and they better have the virtue they need to do it.

There is really no such thing as a necessary occasion of sin but there are many occasions necessitating virtue. An occasion of sin should be defined as the willful dalliance with sin. An occasion of virtue should be defined as an occasion of danger to the soul in a person, place, or circumstance which must be faced by reason of duty or charity. Nuns must be courageous, good people capable of all the sacrifices demanded by these occasions of virtue. The superior who does not train her subjects for these is like a mother who shelters her daughters from every conceivable temptation of the world, from reality, leaving them helpless to meet the normal circumstances of living.

First of all, nuns ought to be given the theological education required by their state. The first religious woman permitted in a Catholic institution of higher learning in America entered there in 1911. Yet even today the religious women competently trained in theology are negligible in number. Few religious will deny that access to competent, qualified spiritual directors is a rarity, yet those priests competent to give spiritual direction find themselves swamped with problems from the idiotic to the incredible, with very few religious ready for any introduction to positive union with God. The number of spiritual books worth reading is also negligible, and the level of spiritual reading in many religious houses is at the level of "The Bobbsey Twins" or "The Campfire Girls." If this were necessary it would be acceptable, but it is not. It is the result of the ingrained belief that if the nun stays out of trouble and does what she is told she will be a saint. It goes without saying that scrubbing floors and pounding a typewriter are beneath the dignity of no spouse of Christ, but to make a virtue of these things when there are so many other more important things to be done is ridiculous. To have a large majority of the one hundred and sixty-eight thousand nuns in the United States supervising in hospitals and teaching mathematics and academic subjects in schools, directing welfare projects under government sponsorship when the teachers of the love of God are nowhere to be found, will be hard to explain. This is not only the religious' field of work, it should be her life. There is no virtue in silencing the inquiring mind, nor is there virtue in depriving minds of the direction and understanding they need if their own life in religion is to make sense to them.

These are provisions that superiors must make if they are to be mothers of their subjects, and there are many more which have not yet been discovered because there has been too little time spent studying all that is involved in the grace of office and the job that could and should be done by those eligible for that grace. No superior questions her obligation to take care of the physical well-being of her subjects; how many think of the obligation to their spiritual welfare? How many actually know or have given much serious and deliberate thought to what is involved in the spiritual welfare of their subjects? Is it a fact that in some communities every material responsibility gets priority over the spiritual considerations which alone form the basis for religious life? There is some room for thinking so when the best brains of the religious orders are dedicated to the management of large hospitals and the administration of academic institutions rather than to the spiritual considerations which are the sole attractions of the finest young people to religious life.

It is the task of superiors to place subjects at work in which they will be most productive for God and souls. Here again, if the superior's attitude is negative her training will take the negative form of protecting them from every danger, even necessary ones. The most talented religious can be held back unnecessarily because of the morbid fears of superiors. If the danger is real, not just in the mind of the superior, if the danger is really great, not just so in relation to the sheltered life of the nuns, it still remains to be determined whether the danger is a necessary one or not. The conservative, frightened mind is wasteful of talent when a danger leads to default in meeting a challenge which should be met, and which if met would develop the person to her full stature.

Living dangerously is not necessarily living foolishly. Policemen, firemen, and soldiers do so but they are not necessarily fools. People find it incredible that a nun in her late twenties is treated as a feckless child in the community when if she were in the world she might well be the mother of five or six children, responsible for the welfare of a husband and a home. It is a scandal to expect greater sacrifices from lay persons for the children they have brought into the world than from religious for their spiritual children. Young girls are going daily to business where their intelligence, humility, chastity, integrity, and will power are challenged more severely than that of religious who by allowing themselves to be cut off from the world get credit for virtue that is not there and could not meet the daily challenges of lay life.

Superiors sometimes appoint subjects to tasks they do not like and often cannot do. Although a superior is a fool to appoint one to a job she is powerless to do, the fact is often discovered only when she fails at it. The real talent of many is discovered only when they are put to tasks they did not think themselves capable of doing. A superior has the duty to use her judgment in this regard and, not being God, she is bound to make mistakes. But to think that a religious should be spared a certain appointment because she does not like it would be to dispense a wife from doing the laundry, a mother from washing diapers, a lazy husband from going out to work. No job in the world offers the luxury of pure joy, and the happiness of most people in their work comes from willingness to do their best at anything to be done. The religious who makes her likes and dislikes the determining factor in her happiness will never find a good superior even if she is standing beside her. It surely is not the grace of office that will assure every nun she will be doing what she wants to do or liking the work to which she is assigned.

It is a grace of office to retire gracefully. Commerce picks out capable young men and trains them for the positions they are later to occupy. Superiors can be considered competent if they have trained their successors. Many business executives hate to see young men of greater ability or acumen appear, for in them they recognize their replacements. However, no board of directors allows this to interfere with the progress of the company. Surely religious whose only interest is the work of God should be as eager to see others do a better job for Him. When a mother or father has done a good job it is a joy for the children to take them into their homes and care for them with love and kindness. There are many things they can do around the house and many ways they can be helpful. They have a tranquillity in their knowledge that their main work is finished and the world is better off in younger, stronger hands. Those superiors are happy, too, in their retirement who see the reins of office in the hands they themselves have prepared for them.

Ignorance of the grace of office makes subjects prone to excuse themselves because of the failings of their superiors. It is very convenient for the religious looking in the mirror of examen to have two standards of judgment, one for the superior and one for herself. But it is dishonest to do so, for truth is always one. The subject is a superior in training and it is a grace of state to ask herself if she is willing to meet the same demands she makes of her superior, to make the same allowances for her superior as she makes for herself. It is so human to complain about a superior who just does not have what it takes, demanding of her something she is powerless to give. Yet who would reasonably expect a hundred watts of light from a fifteen-watt bulb? It is a grace of state for religious to be reasonable. No superior will ever understand or appreciate the grace of office if she has not appreciated the grace of state she had as a religious.

Many say that a good subject makes a good superior, and then go on without any sense of shame to insist that an obedient, docile subject makes a good subject and therefore a good superior. This is ridiculous. No person is good because she is obedient; she is obedient because she is good. The same with the worn-out cliché that if you keep the rule the rule keeps you. The rule is powerless to make anyone good; but good people do keep the rule and it is a measure of the willingness of anyone to be good. The grace of state can, if used, lead a person to goodness; the grace of office can, if used, help a superior to be a good one.

11. Playing It Safe in the Vows

ALTHOUGH human nature does not change it would seem that the age of chivalry is definitely gone. It is not just that the women who insist on replacing men at the lathes of industry are permitted to stand up on the local transit systems. It is not just that women have proven beyond doubt that they are not the weaker sex. It is that the very best, those "who have chosen the better part" and entered religious life, have not shown a very high degree of derring-do after their public profession of the love of God. Love has always inspired glorious deeds. The truer and greater the love the truer and greater the deeds. Religious should be in eager competition with each other to perform these deeds for the glory of the God they say they love. But on the contrary, they seem to have withdrawn from the lists, unwilling to compete, leaving the dragons unslain. They are much more concerned with their own preservation than with victories over the enemies of God and Church.

There is in the average religious a sort of frenzy about avoiding the occasions of sin. She is like the American tourist abroad. She will not travel without first being immunized against every possible disease. Religious worry so much about possible dangers that they are almost too old for the work before they can be trusted in the apostolate. Certainly not too many have been contaminated with the fever of the love of God. Perhaps this fetish for looking after themselves is responsible for the unusual sterility of their lives. Lay people are breaking out with the zeal formerly expected of religious, professionally dedicated people. They are beginning the work they have waited patiently and vainly for their heroines in religion to do. Lay people are clamoring to go to the missions while many religious think they are taking a chance traveling on the Staten Island ferry. Those who love their lives too much do not realize how many ways there are of perishing.

For example, more people are devoured by television than have been eaten by all the cannibals in the world. And when television has finished with them they are no less dead than the bones of the cannibals' dinner. A more positive approach to the problem could eliminate the danger of television as the danger of the cannibals was eliminated, by conversion. Yet Rome had to forbid television in the cloisters or at least severely restrict its use. There is something ludicrous about nuns declaiming against television in the classroom because it ruins the intellectual appetites of the children when they themselves cannot be trusted with it in the cloister. Surely when such restriction is called for, the cause of Christ is lost. How can a job be done by legal device among religious when it cannot be done by virtue? The failure to face this enigma squarely has multiplied the sins of the just. Is religious life a refuge from the occasions of sin? A haven from the dangers of hell? Or is it the opportunity to live for God, to go to heaven with a host of others?

The parable of the talents is so familiar that no one pays attention to it. It is the clearest possible condemnation of playing it safe. It demands that the one to whom much is given produce much. It does not condone people publicly professing to have left all for Christ only to have their arteries closed against grace by the clogging cholesterol of little sins. Christ has no desire to see people forfeit the happiness which should be theirs just because their gift is not total. Religious are not meant to rest on their laurels, to thank God they are not like the rest of men, to write histories telling the world of their own devotedness. The captive Catholic press extravagantly praises its masters' every ordinary deed while the world looks on incredulously at such a strange display of humility. Hardly a single community is ready and willing to, when they "shall have done all these things, say, we are unprofitable servants." It seems no longer a sin of any kind to blow one's horn, the very thing Christ urged His Apostles and followers to avoid. When they gave an alms they were not to go out and blow a horn as the Pharisees did, but they were to do it in secret so that the Father who saw in secret could repay.

While social service has replaced Christian charity, legalism has superseded asceticism. Legalism makes the letter of the law an end while the spirit is abandoned. When this has happened moral theology has replaced ascetical theology as the basis of the spiritual life. True, Christ did first tell the young man that he should keep the Commandments. Yet, when the latter truthfully replied that he had done this from his youth, Christ was unequivocal in His response. He issued a challenge that could not be misinterpreted, that had to be taken up or refused. "If thou wilt be perfect, go sell what thou hast and give to the poor and come follow me." This is hardly for the nun vowed to poverty who has so organized her friends that she wants for nothing. By such action Christ is betrayed daily by those professed to love Him, denied by His elect, doubted by His friends.

The last days of Christ are full of injunctions to love one another. "By this shall men know that you are my disciples, that you love one another. You call me master and so I am. If I being your Lord and Master do these things how much more should you serve one another. He that is first among you let him be the least." Christ gave His followers a strange power, a great power, greater even than that of miracles, the power to love God with their whole hearts and their neighbor as themselves for the love of God. Yet over the past four hundred years, what a metamorphosis has taken place. The cloisters, after years of consecrated effort by courageous and inspired women, were opened to allow the love of God in the hearts of these women to be shared with their brothers and sisters in the world. Now these same cloisters have returned to segregation from the world and — one can and must say it — from Christ living in the world. The pseudo mystics of the day would rather seek God alone at the top of the mount than in the hearts and souls of the sick and poor. Nor can it be said that the laity in the welfare state of the enlightened world do not have need of the ministrations of the nuns. They may not need monetary alms so much now but they need solace and guidance more than at any time in history. They need the hope that comes from friendship with people who have given up the very things which have led these self-indulgent mixed-up people to the extremes of mental anguish. But they are not getting it. They are getting an efficient administration of the benefits of society by hermetically sealed groups with so little in common with the people that they might as well be from other planets.

If the people dedicated to religion were getting what they hoped for by this isolation, the sacrifice would be well made. But they are not. Their lives dedicated to the avoidance of evil rather than the doing of good make the spiritual life of Christianity more like Nirvana than the lighted candle or the city seated on the mountain. The conferences for religious so recently organized have not been called for entertainment. The growing conviction that religious life has failed in one of its essential duties, that of inspiring the young to fill the ranks of consecrated workers for God, has made these conferences imperative. In these, many unpleasant truths have been pointed out which could lead to beneficial changes in the direction of religious life and its better adaptation to the times and needs. But they have raised the opposition of the Sanhedrin, those who refuse to believe they have failed in any way in their administration. It is too painful an admission for religious with little appetite for pain despite their affiliation with the cross. People do prefer to dream. Novels are banned from religious libraries while the life itself becomes a fiction with the praise of God found in the mouth and the heart remaining cold as stone. Unwilling to go all out for God, for truth and the work He would have them do, religious have let their way of life become a protective ghetto from surrounding dangers. And religious lavish praise on the lives of their foundresses without any sense of the contrast to their own. Few communities have kept their fervor, the real life of Christ in the ranks. They are content to expiate their withholding by the unrestricted praise they give those to whom they refuse the true praise of imitation.

It would be consoling if this expiation were motivated by a sense of guilt, default, or failure to measure up. But the lavish praise of foundresses comes from the desire to live off the earnings of the family, to be considered holy by virtue of the habit rather than by the virtue of the person in it. When a nun considers herself better than another because of the community she belongs to, or enjoys the luster coming to her by being a contemplative, she is living off the family, she is a parasite. Judas lived off the purse. Harsh words are needed for harsh times. When married people are called upon for sacrifices unacceptable to nuns, when mothers are more interiorly disciplined than religious and fathers have to work under a strain rejected by religious for their spiritual children, times are indeed harsh.

Many religious are eager for the love of God and willing to pay all for the pearl of great price. But they allow themselves to be badly led by those who have accepted spiritual clichés and even superstitions as principles. Their intelligence has been downgraded and the will stressed to the point where it alone would seem necessary for salvation, as if it were not necessary to know right before doing right. These souls must look up. It is not enough nor even desirable that they seek only the protection of the vows. They must embrace the life opened up to them through the vows, emulate each other in attaining the fullness of life within the framework of the vows. If poverty were a virtue because one had nothing, the world would be filled with virtue. Poverty is a virtue when one gives what he has to the poor, and only this enables the religious to cry out with Simon, "Silver and gold I have not but what I have I give to thee. I say to thee arise and walk." People do not expect any other silver and gold from a religious than virtue and holiness of life. If she does not have these things she is poverty-stricken in the truest sense of that word. She has nothing to give. Chastity is not lovelessness, the inability or unwillingness to love a man. It is the great capacity to love men and women wisely and truly as God commanded them to be loved, rather than for selfish, destructive ends. Chastity is not the virtue of the shy retiring introvert, but of the great of soul eager to love Christ and to find and serve Him in others. Nor is obedience the obsequious servitude of the weakling, the line of least resistance, a voluntary slavery for room and board, a sort of willing residence in a religious concentration camp. The history of the glorious anchorites of Siberia and Northern Russia is filled with peerless sanctity achieved in free, generous response to God, not in the abject acceptance of the inevitable, a single alternative to death from starvation. All that is best in woman is lost when she takes the God-given gift of freedom and hands it back to Him as being too dangerous to use. Who does this merits the verdict of the man who hid the talent in the napkin or buried it in the ground.

There is no real protection in the vows; there is only opportunity. He who loses his life shall gain it; and he who saves his life shall lose it. When the vows represent protection from the dangers to which the ordinary Christian is exposed, then religious life is for the weaker soul; it is for those who can love less rather than those who would love more. For whom the religious vows represent protection rather than opportunity the religious state is meaningless; it is a return to the womb, the express wish that one had never been born.

12. Poverty

PRIEST, brother, and sister are obliged by the same Ten Commandments as the laity. God gave them no special set of commands. There are only the evangelical counsels but these are directives not commands. The only thing religious do is bind themselves with a double onus rather than the single onus of the Christian, who is not bound to less good than the religious. It is ridiculous to think that any Christian can love and serve Christ without a love for the poverty which Christ practiced and recommended. St. John says, "He that hath the substance of this world and shall see his brother in need, and shall shut up his bowels from him; how doth the charity of God abide in him?" The charity (love) must be articulate, and detachment from wealth and riches must be practical; poverty is not a merely philosophical question. Nor is the nun obliged to be more chaste than the single girl in the world. Both are obliged to chastity. The nun is not obliged to be doubly chaste, but doubly obliged to be chaste. Obedience is incumbent on everyone for all authority comes from God, and all are obliged to obey Him. Unpleasant as it may be, wives must obey the reasonable commands of their husbands for he is the head of the house. A religious is no more obliged to obey an unreasonable command of her superior than a wife is obliged to obey an unreasonable command of her husband. For no one can be obliged to go against right reason or her conscience. These are the deciding elements in sin of any kind. Nor does the obligation to respect authority fall any more on the one who is subject to it than on the one who exercises it, but undoubtedly less.

While they have the same obligation to respect poverty, lay persons look to the religious for example and rightfully expect a better performance from her than from the average person. This is quite reasonable, for the very willingness to take the vow indicates a greater basic respect for the material of it, a deeper love for God and greater awareness of a call to a more dedicated way of life. But there are people in the world living more dedicated lives than many religious because of their greater love for poverty. It is a mistake to think that the state in itself makes any appreciable contribution to the personal sanctity of the individual. Some religious simply rest on their oars because of the public profession of vows. But it is the living of the virtue not the making of the vows that determines one's spiritual vitality. Until the vows are seen to be but the threshold of a life of virtue the laity will look in vain to religious for leadership in the love of God.

The failure of the laity to find this leadership can usually be traced to two causes other than the human weakness that walks with men wherever they go. The imbalance between learning and morality is the first. The second is the accentuation of the letter rather than the spirit of the law. Error reverses itself in time, ultimately falling into the error it originally went into error to avoid. Martin Luther insisted that it did not matter what a man did as long as he believed. The average Protestant today considers that it does not matter what he believes as long as he does good. The errors of Protestantism have their counterparts looming just as large in practical Catholicism. Exaggerated moralism leads to the disparagement of man's intellect, and there follows the ridiculous insistence that minor matters assume gigantic proportions. This of course indicates a lack of objectivity and contributes to scruples, mental illness, and general tedium in religion. The exaggeration of pious practices and devotion to trivialities unworthy of a saint but loved by the admirers of the saints have advanced the cause of confusion. The ascent of legalism has led to Talmudic absurdity, to phariseeism. This of course spells death to the spiritual life. Overemphasis is always an abuse. St. Augustine described the restrictions on religious when he said, "Love God and do what you want." True love can never work against the interests of the beloved. It is not true love to abandon all discipline nor is it true love to make discipline itself an end. So the vows can only make religion look ridiculous in the eyes of reasonable people unless from them flows a life of increasing virtue.

In none of the vows is it more important to remember this than in the vow of poverty. For nowhere is it easier to get tied up in legalities, material definitions, splitting of hairs. Poverty and detachment are simply not material for law. They are the material of love. The vow of poverty is not just an escape mechanism for religious from the obligation to provide, but it is the launching pad to the freedom of the lilies of the field so that they can give perfect praise to God, a praise impossible to those cluttered up with material cares. If one shrugs off material cares without using the freedom gained to rise higher to God, but for her own joy and relaxation, the vow is a mockery, a caricature.

There are solemn vows, simple vows, promises, private vows, and the practice of poverty without being vowed to it at all. Regardless of the kind of poverty, the virtue of poverty of spirit is the only fabric which holds these various distinctions together; it is the only thing that can make a man or woman blessed. No matter how poverty is defined it must involve detachment from material things and from the power connected with wealth and its appurtenances. It is folly to say that so many of the abbots of the middle ages, vowed to poverty, yet controlling immense wealth and resources, were better or worse because of their vows. Poverty or the lack of it was in their hearts and in the way they lived their lives. Many poor people are far greedier than the rich because they will do absolutely anything for money. Mink and ermine are no less mink and ermine because they overlay or line the garments of authority. Poverty consists in the motive and the use to which they are put. Even then they can be a great scandal to many who remember that "the Son of man hath not whereon to lay his head." They find ecclesiastical millinery hard to reconcile with this. True, a man's wealth is in his pocket and his detachment is in his heart, but the heart controls the pocket. The vow is a shell unless poverty is practiced, not only in the negative sense of doing without luxuries, but in the sense of doing good works with money, or even obtaining the resources for good works. Can anyone say that the religious who never lays a hand on a coin practices poverty to a greater degree than the man who raises great sums of money and administers them honestly in charity? Granted that the latter is exposed to the temptation to live off the purse, or, even worse, to consider that he has some vicarious ownership over the wealth he has begged for the works he does. But he has a better opportunity of practicing poverty than the recluse living on crusts of bread. There is surely room for both in the plan of things.

Call it a vow, promise, virtue, or anything you wish, poverty must be an imitation of the poverty practiced by Jesus Christ, not just some legal formula to satisfy an ecclesiastical court. Christ did not apologize for giving up carpentry and living off the people, but He lived for the people and died for them too. To live off the people without being at the disposal of the people is a mockery. Whether vowed to poverty or not, the servant of God not denying herself the luxury of superfluous amusement or recreation is not practicing the poverty expected of her by Jesus Christ. The laborer is worthy of his hire, but he is a laborer. He does labor.

Religious are seriously ill spiritually when poverty becomes a measuring stick for all the things they can legitimately possess. Poverty is nothing if it does not actually detach. It is the principle of differentiation between the things one needs and does not need, between the things with which one can be more productive and those which merely distract from duty without providing healthy, normal recreation or rightful respite from the strain of hard work. Such judgments the law cannot make because its job is to determine the extremes. These decisions demand a clear, devoted mind, vision, good judgment, and dedication, qualities which unfortunately few religious have. Through bad judgment and legal confusion, even well-intentioned religious importune the laity for the extravagant use of their time and possessions, blind to the thought patterns created in the laity by these actions. The laity are scandalized at the spectacle of a person thinking herself to be practicing poverty while making use of the very things ruled out by that virtue. They are shocked by the appetite in religious for these things and their irresponsible use of them. To say, "So-and-so is delighted to let us use his car, take his summer home, cruise on his yacht, or give two sisters a trip to Europe" is, with few exceptions, pure "buncombe." It is in fact often some form of "payola," spiritual bribery, or misplaced restitution. When religious have so far lost sight of the needs of others that they can accept all kinds of delicacies and luxuries in their stride, they may have the vow of poverty but they certainly are not practicing the virtue. Few luxuries are procured by religious without some machination indicating an unwarranted attachment. Nor does one have to travel on yachts to be guilty of this. Many a religious moving from one house to another has so many bags and boxes of accumulations that an engineering degree would be helpful in getting them into her cell. Some would just as soon lose their right arm as the trinkets representing their lifeline to the world.

It is senseless to catalog every little offense against poverty. First of all, only the person involved can really say whether there is guilt or not except in cases of such magnitude that there can be no doubt. The only use in listing them would be to show the very young in religion how necessary it is to consider at the beginning of religious life what poverty really means. There will always be the religious string-saver, or the electric nun, unhappy until every switch in the house is off, even the furnace in the wintertime. There will always be the religious peasant with the aspirations and tastes of royalty. But it is better to stress the use to which things are put than to worry about waste, although both equally involve the virtue of poverty. The important thing is not to insist that "this ointment be sold and the money given the poor," but to be sure that her own interests do not dictate what is and is not poverty. Religious have a way of giving up all title to money and its accouterments only to have an inordinate desire to accumulate it for the work with which they are charged. To say that this is only a fulfillment of responsibilities is the sheerest nonsense, for only some form of greed could let things get so out of perspective that their particular charges could assume a priority unwarranted by reality, that money, for instance, collected for the missions could be used for school desks. Nor is it poverty to lay money away for a rainy day when it has no strings attached, rather than pass it on to more urgent needs elsewhere. It is just as much practice of poverty to seek money for the work one is appointed to as it is to refuse it for one's own comfort or pleasure. To enjoy a higher standard of living because of one's appointment is just as much against the vow as it is to refuse to carry financial responsibility because one has no personal use for money.

At no time in the practice of virtue is one dispensed from using her intelligence. Yet there are many religious without the least sense of responsibility materially because the "community" supplies this or that as if there were a printing press for money in the convent basement, or the money spent for these things did not represent the sacrifice of some benefactor. Any number of things can be taken for granted and used wastefully down to light, heat, and water, although it is never a virtue to be penurious. Many a superior has found it cheaper to hire a cook than to have the members of the community do the cooking. Her wages could be paid from what she saved. Of course it is senseless to have a religious do the cooking when she could or should be in a more responsible position, or when her services are more urgently needed in apostolic work. Virtue lies in the middle; laws govern the extremes.

It is the height of folly for any man to try to determine how women should practice the vow of poverty but an example from the world of the male religious could illustrate a point. It is a moot question when the savings of a community by its members giving up smoking would permit the construction of a new building on the campus every few years, whether there is not some obligation on the members to do so. It is a moot question when lung cancer is being attributed more and more widely to heavy smoking, whether religious are not depriving God of their services to some degree by smoking heavily. When the headgear of a community of women has to be washed and ironed by special equipment at considerable expense and inconvenience it is certainly a moot question as to what obligation there is to change it to something more easily handled. When the cloth used in habits, which generations ago used to be cheap because handwoven, is now either hard to come by or very expensive, it is a question whether a community should continue to obtain it for the habit. Poverty would not allow their own sisters to take the time to weave it. Strangely enough, convenience rather than poverty today makes the commercially produced, easily laundered synthetics desirable for religious communities.

A community doing hospital work in a foreign country wore a heavy serge habit. The temperature in one of their large hospitals was around 100 degrees for several weeks in the year and over 90 for a few months. The sisters appealed to their motherhouse to wear a lighter white in their hospitals in tropical climates. The answer they received from their motherhouse was in the affirmative, "IF they wore the white over their serge habits." Is there any thinking person who would not consider this foolishness, among other things, to be a violation of poverty? It was unhygienic; it involved hiring a large number of laundresses; it was hard on the clothing; and it deprived the nuns of much of the vitality they needed in the work they were doing. The poor in those places did not have the clothing available to them in the wintertime that those poor sisters had to wear in the worst heat of the summer. Such contempt for intelligence is never fruitful.

Another community was plagued with malaria. A doctor who had been a member of the order until serious illness forced her to leave, kept seeking large quantities of quinine to treat the sisters. This drug was at that time still the most effective remedy against malaria, even though it had some very undesirable side effects including permanent impairment of the hearing if used extensively. The situation was investigated when it was noticed that malaria was much more prevalent in that community than in others. It turned out, to the horror of all except the members of the community, that the reason for the prevalence was that these nuns were not permitted to use mosquito nets because *St. Teresa of Avila did not use one.* And there were bales of mosquito net going begging. It is incredible that an intelligent woman like St. Teresa would have been credited with tolerating such foolishness in her own daughters. They received no more quinine but a standing offer of all required mosquito netting free. It is inconceivable that such a thing would not be clearly seen as a serious breach of poverty. Not only did the sisters suffer untold pain and fever with serious detriment to their work and prayer, but quinine was expensive and it took a lot of time and care from the doctor. Added to this, the permanent and unnecessary damage done their health should have been seen as willful mutilation.

The tragic thing is not so much that these things happen, but that the nuns are so furious when they are exposed. Few religious have the honest courage to institute the steps required to eliminate these things. One can see the dauntless Teresa walking into that place with a broom and sweeping it clear of foolishness. Conformity has been so canonized in religion that it seems to surpass the vows in importance. Even the Holy Father appeals for realism without too much effect. Poverty cannot be poverty without prudence.

There is no reason for recording these incidents except to underline the condition they reveal. Nor are they isolated cases restricted to small communities. Poverty has only one real value to a religious and that is to assist her to a greater love of God. If after years in religion she finds life purposeless and disappointing she must wonder how she has failed God — if she has not the temerity to wonder why God has failed her. Before coming to any conclusions let her ask herself to what extent she has actually practiced detachment from her own comfort and the luxuries which she herself considered she was forfeiting when she entered religion. There can be little joy in the loveless service of a withdrawn God. But the point of view is important. God usually seems withdrawn because the religious herself has pulled back through her love of material things. God is immutable, there can be nothing withdrawn about Him. The comforts of the world leave a religious confused in her notion of love. Like the young girl who makes the mistake of judging the love of her fiancé by the size of the diamond rather than the size of his heart, the religious does not receive the things she values from God because she values the wrong things. Love is a spiritual, not a physical or emotional thing. It takes so much more love to serve God at the direction of the mind than of the feelings. The religious forgetting poverty still weighs things in pounds and ounces, in time and space; the raiment is more than the body and meat more than the life. So the opportunity for the love of God passes by almost unnoticed, nearly despised.

13. Chastity

ST. PAUL said to the Corinthians, "But we preach Christ crucified, unto the Jews indeed a stumblingblock, and unto the Gentiles foolishness. . . . For the foolishness of God is wiser than men: and the weakness of God is stronger than men."

Most men would insist that you have to be a success to start a world movement, but Christ was apparently content to be a failure and to die crucified. He was asking a great deal of the Apostles in sending them out to sell His product. How could anyone believe that God would really allow His Son to be crucified? Yet they were to do as they were told and leave the rest to Him. Some two thousand years later we know of their success. About the most impossible thing God could ask of His followers would be virginity and chastity. But again, they were simply to take His word and leave the rest in His hands. Hundreds of thousands have done so and thereby given the world all the proof it could want that God has given man the power to overcome himself. To dedicate so fundamental an urge to the glory of God, to abandon man's basic desire to perpetuate himself, for the honor of God, is to prove without a doubt that there is something in the world more important than man himself. The chaste religious by losing herself will find herself; by dying to herself will live. She does this primarily through her vow of chastity. Since her vow is so consequential to herself and the world she lives in, it is very important that she live it well. To do that she must know what she is doing.

Sex, as old as man, basically shared with the animal world, has a new dimension added to it in human relations. For it is possible for man to love. To use sex exclusively for his own pleasure is to debase it, for it is ordained to a higher use. To forego it for the kingdom of God's sake, he must rise to his highest level, a little lower than the angels. There is neither marrying nor giving in marriage in the kingdom of heaven — the only union is with God and it is wider, higher, deeper, and longer than any earthly union could ever be, empowering the vowed to be fruitful in a unique way.

Chastity is the Christian's answer to the slavery of sin; it is lived only through the power of God. Prone to sin and too proud to admit his mistakes or ask pardon for them, man would like to believe that he is enslaved against his will and so incapable of sin and undeserving of punishment. Thus the world is impatient of the chaste who disprove this and tries to convince itself that what they do is unnatural because it is unnecessary. The world wants to believe the only end of man is to enjoy himself and the unusual happiness of those who have given up its prime source of enjoyment defeats it. It is intolerant of them and insists that they don't know what they are doing. So it behooves religious to know what they do if they are to show the world chastity is not a thing they have lightly undertaken.

The full knowledge of what they do and the freedom with which they choose to do it makes their act responsible and essentially human, although divinely inspired. Certainly no man or woman would choose to offer such a thing to God without His inspiration. The burden on religious to be able to give a rational defense of their actions to those seeking an explanation of the life they lead is not really too serious. For the world at large rebels at moral restrictions it chooses to call unreasonable, and certainly the freely taken vow of chastity is one of these. It has not the humor to see that, freedom-loving as it is, it should not really be so concerned about the free renunciation of a personal privilege. The real burden of the religious in knowing what she does in making her vow of chastity lies in the fact that it is a fundamental condition of her spiritual growth.

To take a vow of chastity with every intention of keeping it for life is clearly no small thing. Young people cannot be permitted to make promises of a solemn nature obliging them for life with only a fragmentary knowledge of the matter, or a tendency to overlook the seriousness of what they do through momentary enthusiasm or the impetuosity of youth. This has been widely done through stressing the negative side of chastity and omitting much of the positive instruction needed in the matter.

When the demand for sex education was made by civil authorities prodded by public sentiment, Catholics were generally appalled because of a subtle identification of the sacred with the secret. When sex education in the schools was proposed, Catholic authorities almost everywhere opposed it. Yet the open portrayal of sex in advertising and entertainment today have made it imperative that children be given sufficient information to face with confidence the problems they cannot escape. So the authorities now admit the necessity for sex education for all, with proper qualifications. One of these is that the proper place for fundamental sex instruction is in the home. Priests are preaching this more and more. However, most of these idealists overlook the fact that most parents are not mentally or academically equipped to give the proper instructions, even when their home is a good one. The Church today is insisting more and more on giving the nuns solid theological training to equip them better to give worthwhile religious instruction. Too many pious fables and misinformation were given in times past to young people who found on entering the world how poorly their teaching stood up in the face of critical examination. But part of this theological instruction must be in the facts of life, for many homes are not qualified to send their children out well instructed and the young girls rightly look to the nuns as their second mothers. Where their own parents have not instructed these girls, through unwillingness or inability, the work of the nuns in this field is not only doubly difficult but doubly necessary. Yet of what use can these nuns be when responsible authorities have actually refused them the instruction in chastity that their vows would demand, and have even considered it an occasion to sin to give them the instruction parents should give their children? Surely no nun should be teaching adolescents if she herself has not been trained in the problems of these children and the answers to them.

Chastity has been an accepted part of religious life for so long that it is considered at least impertinent if not insulting to inquire if those taking the vow really understand what is involved. Perhaps the answers to questions about chastity were not so important in times past when many things of importance went unchallenged without dire consequences just because they were part of an accepted way of life. But the children of today live in a time of unparalleled intellectual inquiry. They have received and understand scientific explanations of many things their parents never dreamed about. This has not only made them quite sophisticated but has whet their appetites for answers. They are reasonably less willing to do things just because they have been done. They want to know the why and the wherefore. The traditionalists tend to consider this rebelliousness, but certainly reasoned action is always more meritorious and the questioning of authority brings better administration. When this new determination of the children to have reasons for things is considered bad it is usually because they prod their tired elders into responses they thought erroneously the world was just as well without. The children of today, being so generous with their lives and possessions, cannot be so much worse than the older generation for whom the world was not so transitory, and whose responsibility was so much more personal than social.

The past has tagged curiosity with a morbidity unworthy of this wonderful gift of God. Without it man would have little interest in knowledge even of God. There is a world of difference between honest curiosity and its idle, morbid brother. Religious today have to meet circumstances for which they are unprepared. They have relied too much on tradition in meeting problems for which there was no traditional solution. They must not be asked to rely on the past for answers to be found only in the future. Curiosity is the key to the future. Nowhere is this truer than in the field of chastity. There were certain things one did not ask about, but simply went on taking for granted as one's elders did. When the information needed was finally available, there was unfortunately no longer need for it. The tests of chastity in the modern world cannot be met this way.

The claim that the present generation is on the road to

hell is unreasonable. Things look worse when one grows older, and it takes a special grace and effort for celibates to stay young in mind. It is in the light of accumulated knowledge that the world seems always to be getting worse. People learn more about what has been going on all the time. What teen-ager ever stops to think that his father and mother were ever young and single and went through the process of falling in love with each other and getting married? After all they have been old married people since before the day he was born, a long time indeed to him, all the time he has ever known. Their state has permanence to him; only he is in flux. People think things are new when in reality it is only their knowledge of them that is new. The principles of nuclear physics and electronics are as old as creation but they are new to man. The principles of sex too are as old as creation, but now man, forced to probe deeper into the mechanics of human behavior, finds that real understanding of sex is required for a better performance in life. This is as true for religious as for others; even truer if through foregoing the pleasures of sex their lives are to be more meaningful in service to God.

There is no reasonable excuse for withholding full knowledge of sex from those making the vow of chastity. Yet most religious do not have this knowledge. Any court of the land would consider it illegal to sell something to a client ignorant of what he was getting, with as little knowledge about it as the average religious has about the material of her vow. Lack of sufficient knowledge invalidates the ordinary contract. Yet through ignorance or narrowness, due knowledge is even withheld from many taking the vow of chastity. It is often considered unnecessary and a threat to the peace of mind of the religious by those too small to appreciate the beauty of truth. These erring teachers ask the impossible when they arbitrarily withhold the information many religious need for their survival in chastity.

The attitude of these teachers more than anything else has built the wall around religious for their protection instead of the curriculum of virtue for their proper training. God did not intend religious to teach chastity by running away from the world to protect it, but by living in the same world where people cannot run away. Chastity was not meant to show the power of man but the power of God; where the test seems too great the faith of the man is too weak. Where normal social relationships take on the aspect of temptation too much accentuation has been given occasions of sin; flight and cowardice have become virtues; safeguarding self has replaced the service of others; leaving the ninety-nine in the desert and going after the one that is lost has become not the epic but the novel. Like anyone occupied in work that has dangers, religious should understand the perils and receive the instruction required to meet them. Anything else is dereliction of duty by authority regardless of the reasons for evading this responsibility. Married people practice chastity daily in circumstances considered too dangerous for religious.

Among the facts often withheld from religious by their teachers is the relationship between the emotions and the will. They simply do not know the material of the body or understand it with its muscles, nerves, and emotions. This understanding would keep their life in perspective and prevent either exaggerating or minimizing the problem of chastity. Exaggeration makes every friendship an obstacle to chastity when in reality friendship can be the greatest inspiration to chastity. In fact without it the cloister be-

comes a cold, impersonal place. The prospect of spending her
life in a deep freeze can so revolt a young girl as to make her
flight from religion inevitable. Minimizing the problem can
lead to lesbianism which will be discussed later.

The negative attitude of teachers allows outdated religious
customs to continue long after they have lost all real meaning. Heavy cloaks are worn in chapel for office long after
central heating has been installed. The chemise for the bath
is continued. Nuns laugh at this but in many places it is
still used as a mark of respect for the rule. Few realize that
it was very useful in the times when houses were without
heat, tubs, or showers. Used for warmth, it was continued
under the delusion that it was originated for modesty. To
insist on such a thing for modesty is to make chastity morbid
or, worse, ridiculous. Morbidity in sex must eventually lead
to perversion of some kind.

Morbidity about chastity is very obvious in the concern
about books read by religious. Many priests are asked by nuns
whether they are permitted to read certain books which are
the selection of a Catholic book club simply because they
contain some minor routine involving sex. The religious
with a mature outlook on this matter is considered loose.
Books which any college girl could read without trouble are
considered unfit reading for the nun who directs them. Novels
which could provide a well-earned respite from the tedium
of the classroom and the strain of teaching are considered
occasions of sin instead of honest recreation. This unhealthy
mentality has led to undue secrecy surrounding areas of living
which only open discussion can keep in their proper light.
It contributes to suspicion of every human relationship. It
causes normal childhood experiences to rise as trauma to
haunt unemployed imaginations. It exposes otherwise intelli-

gent minds to scruples. Certainly it cannot help the nuns in their guidance of the young girls for whom they are so often responsible.

Again in error, the imagination has been labeled a very troublesome piece of human furniture. It is unjustly blamed for much of the sexual temptation of religious because of the alluring and seductive pictures it can produce. Yet no one can deal properly with purity without understanding this faculty and the distinction between an impure thought and imagination. The fearful, and they are legion in religion, identify a sensual imagination with an impure thought. They are really very different. Sensual imaginings are inevitable and are not sins; impure thoughts are not inevitable and are sins. People have to think about sex to get the answers they need for normal living, let alone in professions dealing directly with sex. Certainly religious life is one of those professions in which sex must be thought about. These are not bad thoughts but good ones. Bad thoughts are those deliberately engaged in to wrongfully arouse and satisfy one's sexual appetites or desires. The religious for whom sex is not a bogeyman is quick enough to see this difference. The imagination, on the other hand, is never sinful in itself or in its pictures. The imagination has to be hired by the mind, employed by it for this purpose, and be presented to the will before sin is committed. Otherwise it remains like a television set in an empty room. All the pictures in the world flitting across the screen cannot make a sin when there is no one to deliberately watch them.

The imagination gives trouble because it is not put to the work for which it was intended. So it is treated like a bad companion and ostracized. It is only when it remains all day unemployed that it is fresh as a daisy when all the other faculties are crying out for rest. As the faculty of inventiveness it should be at work all day. When it is, it gives minimal trouble as a source of temptation. Whether because of the jaundiced eye of suspicion or not, when the imagination is scorned the religious dooms herself to unimaginative and uninspiring work. How then can she be a leader, planner, or visionary, three roles badly needed in religious life? In considering the imagination as an instrument of temptation, one has to forget that every picture it presents is divorced from reality. This is the reason the escapists draw into it when they cannot face things and make a little world of their own where everything is wonderful. Religious victims of the imagination consider themselves assailed by temptations of the flesh when actually they are only escaping other duties through life in an imaginary world. The "temptations" of the imagination should be ignored as the faker's sales talk about buying a gold brick.

Indirect dealing with matters of chastity is the work of timid, uncertain teachers. This approach is behind the unrelenting burden of work put on the young nun. The body must be put to bed at night just short of sheer exhaustion, as if in this way to avoid lying awake at night troubled with impurity. This is not an argument against hard work but against exhaustion as a protection for chastity. Admitted or not, the indirect approach leads to two serious miscalculations. First, when exhaustion becomes the pattern of one's life much of the zest for living, even spiritual living, is gone. It leaves the mind as well as the body in no condition to deal with the great truths that matter. It leaves the nun undernourished and spiritually hungry after many years of religion. Tragically it is often the most devoted and selfless nuns who suffer this most serious penalty. They are the ones who would profit most by a little leisure to think of God and bear more fruit in the spiritual life. Second, busy religious can falsely conclude that being busy protects them from dangers which only deep thought and conviction can enable them to meet. The old proverb that the devil finds work for idle hands is probably responsible for this conclusion. There are few idle hands in convents but the devil does not give up that easily. It is still his work as the father of lies to deceive, if that is possible, even the elect, and this proverb has been very helpful to him. The devotees of this theory are robbed of the solitude in which they find God in the depths of their own hearts.

Loneliness is a terrible thing. More sins of impurity are committed through loneliness than through lust. Loneliness that is the companion of exhaustion is never really fruitful solitude. The loneliness of real solitude, willingly accepted, affords opportunity for the soul to understand her emotions, and to sort out her real needs from the barking dogs of fallen nature. Few if any of these considerations penetrate the dulled mind of the worn-out nun.

Religious let themselves be misled by the terminology of chastity. "Angelic purity" is a cliché describing this virtue. But it is now and always has been a metaphor, for surely the only ones who can enjoy angelic purity are the angels. This term is so threadbare from use that it is erroneously inferred by many that angelic purity is attainable in this life by human beings. Human purity, human chastity is the very best the nun can hope for. She is not a disembodied spirit any more than she is present in the "remains" laid out in the convent chapel when all her troubles are over. She is body and soul combined, and as such is capable only of actions involving body and soul. Her body must be involved

even in her love for God. This is what fervor means. It is
felt, in the body. When she loves, certain physical actions
and reactions take place in her body whether she likes it or
not, for that is the nature of a human being, a woman. Even
though she should be alert to the warnings that, thank God,
are given by the body in the face of real danger to chastity,
she should never be upset about the normal motions of her
flesh. The emotions themselves are not a danger; they are
the sentinels of the citadel of chastity. Still some insist on
considering them sinful just because the sensation from them
is pleasurable. If there was no sensation there would be no
warning; that this sensation is pleasurable has no special
significance. The hunger expressed in sexual emotion has
no more morality than the emotional expression of hunger
for food. There is a tremendous difference between pleasure
and sin, although many would erroneously identify them.
Ignorance of the physiological makeup of the human person
leads to this misunderstanding.

Nor do the false implications of common teaching on
chastity stop there. Most nuns not only consider that they
can be perfectly pure, but that anything else is mortal sin.
This is wrong. If asked whether she could be perfectly
patient only the presumptuous nun would say yes. Nor
would the ordinary nun think she could be perfectly kind,
perfectly courageous, generous, or unbiased. Perfection in
one virtue means perfection in all. She knows she is not
perfect. Yet if the same nun were asked if she were perfectly pure she would hesitate before answering for she
would think it wrong to admit she was not. She has allowed
herself to believe there is no such thing as a venial sin of
impurity, defect of knowledge or consent usually being
ignored. Yet no human being who is not perfect in any other

virtue can be perfectly pure. Religious are just as impure as they are unkind, impatient, arrogant, disobedient, or imperfect. The mature religious sees and accepts the shortcoming of her nature without undue alarm. She is conscious that she is a sinner. Her effort toward purity is on a par with her effort in the other vitures, nor does she expect any more success in this one than she does in the other equally important ones.

Demanding the impossible of generous and intelligent young people only leads to aridity and coldness, the ultimate abandonment of a senseless pursuit. Who can long interest herself in the unattainable? Angelic purity, perfect purity is unattainable, but chastity is not. Chastity is the willing gift to God of her right to the legitimate pleasures of sex in marriage, while electing to possess her vessel in sanctification and honor. The gift which costs nothing is worth nothing to the receiver. The gift of chastity is a great gift because it costs a great price. No religious should be thrown into confusion because she feels the cost, for nature must groan against the denial of a basic need. Still, the cost should not be exaggerated or dwelt on until it seems impossibly high. Countless people are asked to make the same offering without the same training. In time of war dearly loving husbands and wives are separated without any sure hope of seeing each other again, and are obligated to chastity under circumstances in which perhaps most religious would fail.

In the negative approach to chastity there is always subterfuge. Perhaps subterfuge in many cases has been a woman's only defense even when it is not a very good one. Any nun if asked whether she found her vow of poverty frustrating would not hesitate in saying yes. She would engagingly point out that in giving up dominion over money and its uses one sacrifices many personal pleasures for God. If asked about the frustration of the vow of obedience, with even greater alacrity she would explain the rigors of subjecting oneself to another for life. She would insist that if these vows were not frustrating they would not be worth taking. Yet, when asked if her vow of chastity frustrates her, the average nun pertly replies, "Certainly not!" Apparently it is not ladylike to admit the existence of the sexual urge. And all nuns are ladies to be sure. It appears that the nuns believe that one pure enough to offer her virginal life to God ought not to feel the demands of the nature God gave her, none of the drive for sexual satisfaction for which her body was designed by God. Surely such nuns must consider themselves to be disembodied spirits. If she feels none of these urges the nun is not a woman and therefore is not qualified to enter the convent in the first place. It is rank superstition to believe that with the vow and its accompanying graces there comes an end to the clamor for sexual satisfaction. If such were the case the value of the vow would be nullified by the elimination of the struggle to be pure.

Much has been said about the negative teaching on chastity. There are a few circumstances to be considered in the case. The honest and courageous nuns who had to know the truth have been forced to seek too much of their instruction on these matters from priests. The natural reticence of a good woman and the caution of the good priest lest in his open frankness he give scandal combine to make an inadequate job of it. While some priests are quite competent instructors in the field, and have the good judgment to combine frank openness with reserve and respect, let it be admitted that only a small segment of nuns will be fortunate enough to learn their lessons from such priests. It is foolishness to say this is the work exclusively of spiritual directors or retreat masters, for few convents have satisfactory spiritual directors available, and the dearth of adequate retreat masters is a scandal. The competent ones available are overburdened with the numbers seeking help. In a typical convent fifty religious were directed by a confessor of modest competence who was able to give an hour and a half a week to the fifty. This is not an isolated case. The vast area of chastity has needs for which instruction by priests is not generally available. There should be well-trained competent women for this work. The nuns today have greater need for women in their midst to whom they can turn with trust and confidence for understanding and education in this most fundamental matter.

The women giving such instruction have to be exceptional, with wide horizons, open minds, and a wealth of common sense. They have to accept tolerantly any misjudgment by the Victorians of the community who insist that they survived without this nonsense, which opinion might be controverted by most of their associates. But they also need the understanding support of the authorities in the community who are determined to fulfill their responsibilities to women generous enough to entrust their lives under God to them. It is the sheerest nonsense for priests to be pontificating about personal hygiene for women when there are countless women far better qualified to deal with the matter in every way. It is ridiculous to see erroneous opinions forthcoming from moralists on the use of certain periodic necessities with only their imagination to go on. Surely women can sit down and discuss openly the means of making trying days more profitable. While the morality of these things is nil, so unfortunately is the common sense. But there are women who have not the ability to impart instruction of any kind, let alone that of a very personal nature. They are menaces in the classrooms as well and cannot be totally eliminated, for every profession has its quota of them. But much of the harm they do by rash treatment of a subject beyond their depth could be overcome by making more well-trained people available for such instruction when and where it is needed.

The only sure way to persevere in chastity is the surpassing love of God. But who loves God without a love of knowledge? When there was unquestioning respect for authority it was enough for the kingdom if the king knew what he was doing. Now every man is a king in his own right; he democratically demands some say in decisions and reasons for anything he is asked to do. Who will say he is wrong? Is there not more merit when something is done with full knowledge and consent? Can consent be full without full knowledge? The religious cannot be asked, in fact must not be permitted, to make a vow of chastity without knowing very well what she is doing, what is and will be required of her. For chastity without question holds the key to the problems of human behavior in the future. To gain the attention He needed for His words, Christ worked miracles for the people. Today, to gain the attention she needs for her teaching, the Church uses the miracle of man overcoming himself through chastity. Chastity meant nothing in the days of Christ for it was unknown. But today, when chastity is freely vowed and lived by intelligent, dedicated people, the attention of the disbelieving world is focused on them.

In our day the world has seen the greatest armies of all time assembled and the greatest weapons of destruction invented. The victories for which these armies fought and won quickly melted away in the peace which followed, for the simple reason that the same man who could vanquish his enemies could not conquer himself. This amazing man who will soon have harnessed the elements for his purposes has not learned control of himself. He cannot be chaste; he does not want to believe it is natural, let alone possible. The victorious without self-discipline have nothing to offer the vanquished but the backs of their hands. For they, after their victories, cannot wait to return to the worship of their own pleasure in which they spawn the seeds of their own destruction. Few are found to dedicate themselves to peace through victory over self.

The life of dedicated chastity never carried a more important message for the world than it does today. But that message will never reach the world unless those vowed to chastity know clearly what it is all about. Let us face it, the majority of them do not. Saying one's prayers and frequenting the sacraments is not enough preparation for chaste living. These practices must be buttressed with the knowledge required to meet the trials, and this knowledge involves the natural as well as the supernatural means of chastity. While the knowledge and love of God are the basis for making the vow of chastity, the knowledge of self is the basis for keeping the vow. The ordinary religious subconsciously looks on grace as a sort of high-powered soul fuel poured by God into the head of the one who loves Him. But grace is a strength from God which builds on nature and comes through circumstances of persons, places, and things, as well as through the normal channels. Grace does not specially enlighten the woman who refuses to take the ordinary channels of enlightenment. It is tempting God to expect to be chaste when she does not even know her own body, let alone understand it. The human body must be understood by the apostolic nun who wishes to persevere in chastity.

Sex is a very important five to eight percent of any person's life. Those who think it is larger than that need only consider the amount of time the normal person gives directly or indirectly to it. If at times the nun is bothered more than at other times, she should learn the mechanics of sex and accept it for what it is, not letting her frustration flow into other fields of her work. She should know that she is more of a woman because she has these troubles than if she were spared them. The upsetting occasions when her feelings may run riot should be used calmly as inspirations to renew her vows as an expression of her love for God above all others. She should under no conditions push the panic button or give in to the widespread, silly temptation to think she is any different from the other nuns around her. Her needs are not greater or less than theirs, and she will only appreciate this when the nun's instruction covers the physical makeup of her body and the purpose of her God-given faculties and organs. She should understand the physiological and psychological aspects of chastity both in regard to her own and the married state. Knowledge of the latter will protect her from the ridiculous tendency of some religious when assailed with sensual urges to consider marriage as the answer to all these problems. It will also help her to avoid thinking of the married state as somewhat degrading insofar as the animalistic side of it might be considered beneath good people; she will see it as the poorest defense mechanism, as if the marriage act were not a wonderful part of true love for those whose privilege it is.

The unrealistic defense mechanisms of religious are like the famous guns of Singapore, their hugeness so comforting as they pointed out from shore. They were useless when the enemy eventually attacked from the rear by land. Religious coming from good homes with exemplary parents, and never having to endure the trials and disappointments of the normal marriage, can consider marriage very attractive when the trials of religious life are upon them. While the honest nun must admit the sexual frustration that is hers in religious life, she must not be deceived by the juvenile and delinquent philosophers of sex into thinking that there is less general sexual frustration in the lives of married people in the world. The high incidence of divorce and separation indicate the number of married people unable to find the satisfaction in marriage which they had expected. Many married people are required to practice a higher degree of chastity than many religious for they are often exposed to greater temptations against the virtue. Who can doubt that the man who has a carping, critical, uncooperative wife at home, but a lovely, devoted, and capable secretary in the office, is more tempted to sin than most religious? It is generally more difficult to mingle with people in the world and live chastely than it is to remain faithful to the vow, withdrawn from the world in a cloister.

The religious feeling the pinch of chastity thinks of marriage in the abstract and might easily be convinced that in the abstract it is a more reasonable approach to God than chastity. But she cannot get married in the abstract to some knight in shining armor. Many women may love the man they marry but not too many marry the man they love, their first choice. Nor do the joys of marriage in most cases compensate for the trials, disappointments, responsibilities, and crises. Nor does a wife have much choice of the corporal penances she will undertake. By the time she has looked after the children, cleaned the house, made the beds, done the washing, prepared the meals, and listened to the complaints of her husband on return from work, she hardly feels much appetite for penance. It is very debatable whether the frustrations of religious life compare to those of marriage. Few married women of any spiritual stature have not wondered why they did not choose the better part even though they would have made no better nuns than wives.

The penalty for her ignorance of sex is the rejection by the nun of the essential power given the Christian by Christ, the power to love. This leads to love being feared as a threat to chastity rather than esteemed as its best defense. The nun is not chaste because she does not love a man, but she is chaste because she loves God more than any man. The lovely housewife in the presence of the attractive husband of the woman next door is not chaste because she does not like the man next door but because she loves her husband more. A good woman never does anything to destroy a love which means a lot to her. She could not destroy the greatest good of one she truly loved, his relationship with God. This would be doing the beloved the greatest possible harm and could not pass for love by any standard.

The woman who has little capacity for loving a man will not have much capacity for loving God, for her real love is herself. The woman who would make a good wife and a good mother would generally make a good nun for she has the basic requirement — goodness. The femininity and goodness required for either position is about the same. Any doubt about this can be laid to looking for greener grass on the other side of the fence. Human nature inclines everyone to compare the difficult features of her life to the wonderful features of her neighbor's. It is a form of self-pity. The good woman gets married and makes the best of things. The nun with troubles would do well to follow her example. If she cannot face the problems of religious life she will hardly have more courage to face those of marriage. Of course there are always exceptions and the Church has made provisions for those who change their minds, though a large quota of these are just people with a large capacity for unhappiness.

The basic requirement for a nun is that she be a woman. A woman needs a man; she will always need a man. She is made for a man, although the longer she lives without a man the less demanding will be the need. If by vocation she chooses to go through life without a man she must be prepared to pay certain penalties, accept certain frustrations. Facing these squarely and dealing with them calmly is the way to keep them in perspective. They are never so impossible to handle as when they are not admitted. Many fail in chastity not so much from lack of grace as from ignorance about what is involved in being chaste. These are the ones who are sent from religious training like sheep before ravening wolves. They have been discouraged from thinking about the things they should know, when this thought could save them in the time of danger when thought is all but impossible. Few religious walk wantonly into sin but many find themselves in an occasion when it is all but too late to cope. Only the wicked walk deliberately into sin but the innocent can be taken by surprise. God's grace and protection are never wanting but He does not multiply miracles.

There is no replacement for the positive approach to chastity for religious working in the world. Nuns have too often been considered chaste when they were really only cloistered. Having willingly segregated themselves from the world, they simply lack opportunity to be unchaste. Chastity is not developed under these circumstances. The lack of this virtue more than anything else was responsible for the failure of the priest-worker movement. The training they had simply did not warrant the chances they took. Their chastity was not equal to the job; they overestimated their virtue.

If a nun is going to associate with men in her work — and in active work what nun does not? — she must be chaste, not just sheltered. Many young people attending schools taught by priests, brothers, and nuns together are shocked that there is no association allowed between them. If priests and nuns with vows of celibacy and chastity cannot associate together in their work without sin, how can young people in the world be expected to court and marry without sin? Such thinking would consider courtship without sin an impossibility.

A woman needs a man, and a nun is first of all a woman. She must never be allowed to think she will not love the men she works with. If they are the least bit lovable she cannot avoid it. Some of these women become emotional shambles when they first realize that they do love these men. Unless they are very honest and have someone competent to turn to in utter candor, they may be quite shattered by the experience. A good woman meeting a good man will certainly love him. It is inevitable. She simply loves the lovable. When she tries to tell herself she does not, she either lies or allows herself to be deceived by wishful thinking. Nuns glowingly admit their love for the little waifs they tend, for the human wrecks they care for in social-welfare centers, for the unwed mother, the hobbling aged, yet they cannot admit their love for younger, finer men, pillars of the Church, truly interested in being good. They are afraid to do so when they should see, if they love the former, that they could not help loving the latter, for there is ever so much more reason for doing so. The nun foolishly feels she would be violating her vow at least in her heart if she loved one or more of these men, when she would actually be violating Christ's command if she did not love them. No Christian should ever be ashamed to love people. She should be ashamed if she does not. There is danger for the nun who would believe she does not love such people only to learn in a moment of emotional stress that she had deceived herself. The nun candidly admitting that she loves someone is protected by her virtue which outlines the behavior demanded by her love of God. In this behavior is contained all the mortification demanded for her salvation.

Many a good married man who is forthright and honest knows he loves his secretary. She is a good woman with many admirable qualities, devoted to him and his interests. Should he dislike her? This man is good not because he does not love his secretary but because he loves his wife and would not put anyone else's interests before hers. His secretary may cause him more emotional upset than does his wife but that should be expected, for he has to be more careful with her than he does with his wife. Conjugal love which becomes routine after a few years is not less deep because it is less emotional. This honest man sees the true picture. Because he is devoted to his duties he can cope with this situation. Being the type of man he is, he is not only lovable but he has also developed a great capacity for loving others as well. Because he has good judgment, the people he loves are good people. He values their goodness above all else and so he preserves and respects it precisely through his love for them. These people, chaste enough to overcome their own small desires, have a tremendous influence on others. Who needs this influence more in her work than the nun? But to have it, she must understand herself, her own body, and practice self-discipline. Obedience to the rule does not give her self-discipline but conformity. If she relies on it where she needs self-discipline, she will get as much support as she would walking into an open elevator shaft. The rule to be observed in associating with those she loves is simple enough. Her friendliness must be without familiarity, neglect of duty, or scandal. This of course does not mean the pharisaical scandal of the jealous. Her love must be based on the principle of self-sacrifice. It must be a Christlike love. Those incapable of this have no place in religious life or the apostolate. The work of Christ demands the love of Christ.

The nun must be a woman. A woman wants children. Religious or not, this is her destiny, which she either fulfills or is frustrated in an essential feature of her life. This is the reason the nun leading a sterile life is unhappy. Since through her vow the possibility of having children of her own flesh and blood is precluded, these must be replaced by adoption. Her love for God will bear fruit in the spiritual children of the apostolate. If she does not want children — and strangely there are some women to whom the idea of having children is repulsive — she lacks something very essential in a woman and to the work of a nun. The married woman who through no fault of her own is sterile often finds her husband frustrated and herself dispirited by the fact. There is a compulsion on most childless couples to adopt children. It is not primarily for what they can do for the children, but because their love is meaningless if it does not find completion in the care of the fruit of their love. Since the love of the nun should be even greater than that of the woman in the world, her need to reproduce herself in children will be greater. That she wants these children primarily as proof of the fruitfulness of her love for God does not lessen her need of them.

It is the basic desire of every human being to be loved. This is what makes it so strange that so few are willing to cultivate the goodness which alone can make them lovable. It is equally strange that those wanting to be loved so much make such little effort to acquire the selflessness which determines their capacity for loving others. Chastity cannot be a positive virtue in anyone without goodness and selflessness. Without it how can the command of Christ that His followers love one another be fulfilled? It cannot be. Yet those refusing to do as He commanded prefer their own judgment to His. He does not command things vainly nor does He thrust anyone unprovided into danger. How then can any religious consider life without even friendship a success? Who makes a better friend than the saint? The communion of saints is the most intimate union of friends, not some vague amalgamation reserved for eternity. And it begins and exists here and now between living members of the Mystical Body. It is an integral part of religious life. Thus the lovable nun is loved by her friends and envied by her enemies. Her chastity grows in her love for others; it is the virtue setting the good of others above one's own sensual desires. True friendship enables her to rise to the heights of immolation.

The world desperately needs evidence that chastity between friends is possible. It seriously doubts the possibility of two people loving each other without indulging their sexual appetites, if it has not disclaimed that possibility altogether. It refuses to concede that sensual love is really only self-indulgence. The ability of religious to love truly and deeply but chastely is the proof it needs. Thus it is unfortunate that among religious there has been such wide-spread "unqualified" prohibition of "particular" friendship. Inordinate friendship is undoubtedly "particular," but all particular friendship is certainly not inordinate.

How can particular or special friendships be wrong when Christ Himself so preferred John that the latter could refer to himself as "the disciple whom Christ loved"? When He plainly selected Peter and James and John for special privileges, without apology? When Lazarus, Mary, and Martha were known as His particular friends?

Obviously particular friendships are not wrong; inordinate ones are. Our Lord was not embarrassed that Mary Magdalen clung to His feet after His resurrection, nor that she dried His feet with her hair before His death, nor that John leaned on His bosom. Nor did He feel any necessity to apologize to Martha for dispensing Mary from the chores since she had chosen the better part. He did not send her back to the kitchen just to make things look right.

The same trouble exists among religious as among people in the world. If this one is not enjoying a friendship then no one else can enjoy one either. This, regardless of the fact that, to be enjoyed, a friendship must be a good one. There are certain people who are just more lovable than others, who attract more and better people to them. The nun who is unwilling to make the sacrifices necessary to be lovable resents this. Like the bereaved mother before Solomon, she hopes to solve her loss by having the other woman's baby cut in half so neither will have anything.

In the matter of friendship it is time that someone clearly exposed the fear underlying friendship between nuns. The fear is that, deprived of the normal association with men and the normal satisfaction of marriage, the religious women who form friendships will, as the days grow long and the Lord is long acoming, tire of unmanifested love and seek the forbidden pleasures of homosexuality. This is so, and let none deny it. But who ever mentions such a thing? There is a very strict rule in all religious houses of men or women covering the solitude prescribed after the grand silence at night. So strict is this rule in seminaries that the students are told that if they are caught without authorization in the room of another student during the grand silence they will be expelled without recourse. The reason is seldom given, however, for this special strictness. Most are allowed to think that it is solely to preserve recollection for the meditation of the following day. That is, all but those who have reason to know why it is so strict — the homosexuals. Morbid fear banishes from the cloister the deep friendships which inspire souls to the heights of selfless charity, while the same fear at the same time drives ignorant souls of weaker mold to the edge of perversion without warning.

The reason this rule is so strict is that, if one person is found in the cell of another after lights out, during the grand silence, it is assumed that he or she is a homosexual. A homosexual is one who can find sexual satisfaction in actions performed with a person of his or her own sex. Homosexuality is physical love between two people of the same sex. Let it be understood that it can exist in any convent of appreciable size. As soon as the fact is faced, the incidence of it will be kept at the lowest possible degree. That the vast majority of religious are unaware of its existence does not eliminate it. Ignorance deprives the innocent of the protective grace of knowledge. Like all human failings it will never be completely eradicated, but when discovered it should not be allowed to continue simply because those in authority wish it were not there. The subject should be thoroughly discussed as part of training in chastity. It is only pride — rank, rotten pride — that keeps it from being aired openly. Religious need the protection of knowing about it.

The genuine lesbian or female homosexual is the woman with no interest whatsoever in the opposite sex. She can be fully stimulated by her own sex. She is not necessarily the masculine type; she can be very feminine and demure. Nuns who know the girl in school who easily gets crushes on her teachers might be apt to think this is the type. Not necessarily. Crushes are a normal passing fancy with most adolescent girls. The lesbian is never boy crazy and is happiest when with the girls. The world of men is not revolting to her; it is just not interesting. Nor need a lesbian be actually committing sin, though she usually does sooner or later. There are homosexuals who recognize themselves for what they are and undertake to live a good moral life with practiced discipline. The big difficulty with a homosexual in a convent is that the occasion of sin is everywhere around her. If she is not an emotionally controlled person with a high degree of understanding of her problem, she is certainly living in the wrong environment to save her soul, to say nothing of the occasion of sin she would be to the bisexual weakling. The bisexual is the person who is prone to indulge in sexual sins with either sex, being stimulated by either. She is the kind who engages in love affairs with other girls when boys are not available, or even when there is a girl who can excite her more than the boys available.

The question naturally comes to the average nun to whom

much of this may be a complete revelation — why would such a person think of entering a convent in the first place, let alone take a vow of chastity? The answer is not quite as difficult as it might seem. The potential homosexuals who enter religion are usually good people who don't quite understand themselves, who want to lead good useful lives and save their souls. But the normal sexual aspirations are just not theirs. This can be due to a mixture of the genes, or more commonly to a home environment in which for some reason or other they were not brought up normally. Perhaps the mother was intolerant of the sexuality of the father and considered the whole business of sex rather revolting, and her secondary passive role in the act a sort of prostitution. The reaction of the girls in the family (usually one) to this was contempt for men and reliance on the company of women from whom they were inclined to get their understanding, sympathy, and love. This person in the convent need not be a practicing homosexual, but the chances are, when she runs into misunderstanding or persecution, real or imaginary, she will turn for consolation to someone of her own sex, indulging in a love affair of some kind even though it may be within the bounds of propriety. She is always a threat.

Lesbianism is usually found in the emotionally immature. Those who have these inclinations in the convent should be dismissed whenever discovered. But they should not be confused with the pseudo lesbian or the nun who, to prove her chastity to herself, develops an antagonism toward men. She is one of those women who deeply resent interference in the life and work of any nun by any man at all.

The figure accepted for homosexuality has been generally 3 percent of the people. But in recent years because of further research and investigation this figure has been revised to 10 percent. Many think the problem is on the increase, but others consider that there is just more frankness about it now and therefore it is coming to light more frequently. It is a problem as old as man. What should be done about it? It should certainly be brought to the attention of the authorities. True, there are times when it cannot be. Sometimes authorities are not competent to deal with it, either through their lack of sympathy with those involved, or because they are apt to consider the whole thing an indictment of their administration. Then they are inclined to act more from hurt pride than from a genuine concern about the problem. It should generally be brought to the attention of authority, however, and steps taken to protect the innocent. The real protection against it comes from knowing that it exists and from bringing it to open discussion so that anyone can recognize its early symptoms.

Friendship between nuns is no more than should be expected, but a sweetheart relationship is another thing. Whenever two nuns are seen holding hands, lavishing endearments on each other, particularly caresses of any kind, there is always room for legitimate suspicion. The exchange of love letters which anyone would recognize as such is another indication. Many people resent any two nuns being friends and wishing to talk privately, but this is wrong. There is room for such friendships in the convent. But when the same two people persistently exclude all others, or neglect their duties to be with each other, or do not respond in charity to the needs of others, there is room for considerable thought. If they are not lesbians they are certainly involved in unworthy indiscretions. They are not exercising the charity required by community life.

Much remains to be said but this is sufficient to bring the matter into the open. There is one thing that must not be taken for granted. Sometimes a sister can be physically aroused by another. If this happens now and again, little or no attention should be paid to it. It is no more than normal. Ordinary precautions should be taken against physical familiarities without undue upset. It is only when this is persistent and one seeks the other's company on almost any and every pretense that there is real danger. The great dangers of these friendships are among the ungenerous who have lost their enthusiasm, if they ever had any, for the lives they are supposed to lead. They are simply content, without leaving the convent, to take what satisfaction they can find in friendship along the road. It rarely happens among those whose desire to love God is paramount and who are generous in their response to the chores of the day or the position they have.

Surely if anyone is capable of a good, healthy, helpful friendship it is the religious vowed to chastity and practicing it over the years. If religious have to be more careful than others it is a clear admission that their chastity results more from a lack of opportunity to do wrong than from real virtue. The nun should be vigilant; knowing the conditions of her life and the dangers to be met, she should meet them with more virtue than the ordinary person. She has a higher goal in life and greater awareness of the ever-presence of God and therefore should be safer in almost any undertaking.

Many a religious does not know what chastity really means until she comes to love someone very deeply and truly. Faced with a challenge, she must either forego her love for God as the first interest in life, or love this person within the framework of her love for God. She is very solicitious that such a love on her part will contribute to the honor and glory of God, and the effort to be sure that it does accounts for the greatest purity of action in her life. The religious of the negative school very often roots out such a friendship as something dangerous, and when she does, out goes the wheat with the chaff. It takes some discernment to see that it is impossible not to love a person deeply when Christ is plainly dwelling in her soul. Such has been the basis of the greatest loves in the world by the purest people. These people through true love rose above the most clamorous demands of their human nature.

Nothing final can ever be written on the subject of chastity. Much thought has to be given the subject, and much more thorough treatment by more competent people. However, it goes without saying that the more the religious knows about what she does when she takes her vow of chastity the more truly she honors the God for whom she takes it. The chaste religious, the most lovable person in the world, symbolizes the heights to which men can rise without ever denying their need for love and their capacity for loving.

14. Obedience

In ANY study of religious life the question of obedience looms very large. Obedience represents the arena of man's struggle with his worst enemy, pride. Through disobedience man falls and dies; through obedience he rises and lives. Therefore, religious or not, man must obey. The religious only adds to her obligations the vow to obey the legitimate authority she freely accepts.

The problem with obedience is its interpretation in any given circumstance. When and in what circumstances must a person willingly do the bidding of another under God? Actually in this matter, as in all other matters, the individual conscience must reign supreme. No one sins who does not deliberately go against her conscience. Granted, her conscience must be a true one, but in the last analysis it remains between the soul and God to know whether that state of truth exists or not. Rules and regulations of any kind must admit of exceptions, must remain within the realm of reason. No one disobeys unless she does violence to her conscience or knowingly and willingly goes against right reason. These things cannot be separated from the vow of obedience. It is necessary in any discussion of the subject to throw as much light as possible on conscience and right reason in relation to obedience.

Obedience, then, is the freely accepted obligation, under pain of sin, to accept one's religious superiors as the representatives of God, and to obey all their reasonable commands, within the limits of their authority. Nothing will be said in this chapter which does not fit that definition.

Of course, no one will question that the vow must be freely undertaken. The issue, therefore, relates to superiors as the representatives of God, and to the reasonableness of their commands. Certainly obedience depends on the authority which comes from God — and there is much to be said about the one who represents God in the life of another. As for the word "reasonable," many would have it omitted because of their zeal for detailed, blind obedience. But if the word "reasonable" is omitted, there is no matter for obedience, because the act being thus considered is not a human act. Only human acts are the matter of obedience, and to be human, acts have to be reasonable.

Those who would omit the word "reasonable" make the fourth commandment the complete treatise on obedience. Yet the determination of what is reasonable, and how far any individual subject or superior can go in her own judgment about the reasonable, is what makes for the detail and the length of this discussion. It is not enough to say that if almost everyone holds the same opinion the individual should capitulate to the general judgment. It is not sufficient to say that superiors are right just because they are superiors. Thomas More and Bishop Fisher stood all but alone in refusing to take the oath of loyalty to Henry VIII. Thomas More's wife and daughter questioned his wisdom and implied plain stubbornness, considering the number of bishops and priests signing the oath. Yet everyone knows where Thomas More and Bishop Fisher are today, while the world must wait to learn the judgment of a merciful God on the majority of bishops and priests in Reformation England.

In spite of all the commentaries, constitutions, and commentaries on constitutions, no superior can expect or command a subject to go against her reason. What is reasonable to her is what, in her honest and best judgment, is reasonable. She does not have to be right, but she must honestly believe she is. She simply has to use the best judgment she has, and be willing to follow it until she sees she is wrong, or at least doubts that she is right. Nor does this leave too wide a scope for private interpretation of obedience. It does not make obedience a matter for caprice. Even though God made salvation an individual matter, no one goes capriciously to heaven or to hell. The injustice of superiors is not magically made justice by their position, nor does craven love of security dispense the subject from representing to superiors what her right reason tells her any good woman would be grateful to receive.

Obedience must leave with the individual the challenge to obey, the opportunity to avoid going wrong through error, bad judgment, vanity, or pride. This is the challenge to virtue and it remains, and must remain as God made it, a challenge to the free individual which no amount of legislation can remove. Religious do not voluntarily sign themselves into corrective institutions where their freedom is left outside the front door.

The matter of obedience is fundamentally one of loyalty to God, fidelity to God. It is only within the framework of this loyalty that loyalty to oneself, the community, its rules and constitutions, makes sense. If there is true loyalty to God there can never be disloyalty to community or self. The contrary idea would only come from placing *the holy rule* on a higher pedestal than Sacred Scripture or God Himself. The foundresses of various congregations and their dedication to God are always invoked when reverence for the rule is urged. But one thing should be clear. Although these people were incredibly loyal to God they were generally discontented with the status quo, and their communities live after them to prove it. They loved God and their loyalty was to God. Thus they refused to accept the platitudes of those who insisted that they get in line and accept things as they were. They listened much more to the inner voice of God than they did to external forms. Because of their true love of God and their objectivity, the inner voice came through very clearly. St. Joseph was no dreamer, but so attuned was he to the inner voice that he was prepared to obey God's message in a dream without hesitation or fear of being wrong. The foundresses were not too concerned that they appeared not to obey men for they knew how poorly men obeyed God. However, it was their willingness to obey which made them great and kept them safe. Apparent opposition was their great cross, and on it they sacrificed their good names and even their peace of conscience. Like Christ they were accused of blaspheming the beloved and eternal Father. There was only agony for them in doing as they did, but they knew God had to be obeyed, and their pride was conquered through their obedience.

Many of them were not obliged by religious obedience because they founded their great works before becoming religious. Their obedience was to the bishops and other authorities under whom they worked. Their works were frequently blessed because they persevered in their convictions while submitting under obedience to the contrary, convinced that God in His own good time would enlighten the minds of those who opposed them. And so it happened. They would be the last to demand slavish and unreasonable obedience of their followers. This was the work of lesser souls who followed them. Nor would it be much consolation to a foundress to know that the only reason being given for things her daughters did was that they had been done that way for so many hundreds of years. Their own greatness came from their ability to read the signs of the times and make the changes required.

Obedience that does not produce humility is not obedience. It may be obsequiousness, servility, respect of persons, or simply a case of looking after one's own interests, but it certainly is not obedience. The purpose of obedience is the conquest of pride and atonement to God for the disobedience of man. Such atonement is very reasonable, as everything undertaken by men in the name of God must be. To do unreasonable things in the name of God is a greater sin than pride; it is to blaspheme.

The practical problem of obedience is to decide what "reasonable" means. There are many factors involved in the answer. Some have been dealt with in other chapters, for example, emotion and reason, for who cannot be misled by her feelings? Good judgment and objectivity are also involved as are honesty and generosity. What has been said in those chapters need not be repeated.

There is no greater apparent conflict than that between reasonable and "blind" obedience. Blind obedience can be defined as the immediate acceptance of the commands of a superior, without qualification, question, or reservation, as the will of God. Some think that blind obedience is unreasonable. Right here and now let it be said clearly that if it is unreasonable, it may be blind but it certainly is not obedience. The problem is not so much the blindness as the inclination of the proud to consider something unreasonable because it is not understood. Atomic energy is not understood by many people, but who would call it unreasonable? Blind obedience is the highest kind of obedience made unreasonable only by those who do not, or better, will not understand it. It is the mark of the saint, and if there is one thing the saint is not, it is blind. She sees with a clarity not widely shared. It is this very clarity which enables her to avoid in blind obedience anything unreasonable, or anything unworthy of God, the ultimate authority on whom all obedience depends. Such is the union of the saint with God that she immediately senses the unworthy. Only she is really capable of blind obedience who is not blinded by her passions to the truth, whether it comes from her own enlightenment by God or the enlightenment and inspiration of her superior by God. The reason for this is simple enough. The closer she is to God the quicker her recognition of objective truth. This was the blind obedience of St. Joseph which set him on the road to Egypt.

The old *Lives of the Saints* tended to "prove" the sanctity of the subjects by extolling their blind obedience in things which many would consider quite unreasonable, even idiotic. This tradition has helped to promote an unreasonable obedience. But many of these records are highly doubtful, devotional or apocryphal, certainly not very authentic or historical. They are traceable to sources hardly qualified to pass on things as theological as sanctity. Many of these tales edified believers but made cynics of honest infidels. An example of this type of thing is the life of St. Francis Xavier, for years the idol of aspiring young missioners. Generations of missioners took it for granted that he had the gift of tongues,

through which he brought millions into the Church. However, the honest research of Father James Broderick brought
forth an excellent biography of the saint in which it was
clearly stated that no acceptable evidence had been forthcoming that the saint had the gift of tongues. On the contrary, there was much good evidence to indicate that he
had great difficulty with the languages of the people to whom
he went. These old wives' tales are a great source of discouragement for missioners who find the problems of foreign
language all but insurmountable. The later apostles would
have found their lot much more tolerable, and the inspiration of Francis Xavier more efficacious, if they had known
the truth. Not having the gift of tongues, he did share the
very difficulties they met and became a saint because he
persevered through them all.

The vow of obedience must be studied from the points
of view of both superior and subject. For, although obedience has usually been related to subjects, obedience has a
twofold obligation, on the superior first, and then on the
subject. The authority of superiors has been built up over
the years on the well-founded assertion that they stand in
the place of God; undue emphasis has led to the point where
they have all but eclipsed Him. Many superiors have absolved
themselves from their foolishness simply because they had
a right motive, without adverting to the insult of attribut-
ing a stupidity to God. No one who has thought of her
obligation of wielding authority in the name of God rather
than the subject's obligation to obey in the name of God
could commit such a folly.

The priest going to the altar to offer the sacrifice of the
Mass assumes a burden made possible by his faith that the
arrangement was instituted by Jesus Christ. It ill behooves

him to forget how presumptuous his action would be under any other circumstances. Nor should he ever say Mass without deep concern for his unworthiness. It is no small thing to act in the name of God. However, the superior who is so very prompt to warn the subject about whose power she wields should be at least equally prompt to remind herself that her actions should be as worthy as possible of the authority she invokes. Religious teaching school find the most insubordinate and unmanageable children coming from broken homes where the parents have little respect for God and less for each other, where the influence of one parent on the children is daily undermined by the other. The religious ruled by superiors acting in a way totally unworthy of the God they claim to serve develop the same religious rebelliousness and anarchy as the unmanageable children of the classrooms.

The title "sister servant" does not make the superior so in fact. There are superiors who have in their heads a library of information on the obligations of subjects but are blank about the obligations of superiors. Few crises have arisen in the Church which are not connected directly with the abuse of authority. The crisis in the Church and the religious state today can be traced to the same thing. The crisis is more in authority than in obedience. The problem originates with the superiors, the first pole of religious obedience.

Most of the thinking behind the appointment of a superior is negative. Too few of them are chosen because they are the outstanding people for the job. They should know this, but many consider themselves to be appointed directly by God just because they were appointed through no machinations of their own. Since they did not want the job or openly campaign for it, it is the work of God. It certainly is, but not in the way the average superior looks at it. It is the work of God because He did determine that it was poor weak human instruments who would rule His Church. But beyond that most of the appointments are due to the desire of major superiors to carry out their own theories through loyal followers. True, most major superiors would not think it out that clearly, but they are human, and few men and women in history have been objective about themselves.

Thanks be to God, the most venal superior elected or named through the most unworthy means cannot by herself wholly frustrate the work of God in the souls of others. God will always make an abundance of grace available even to her for the good of the work being done, and to the religious involved for their own souls' progress. But this again is from the negative point of view. Positively, the superior must try to exhaust all her natural talents and be as open as she can to the grace of God in all objectivity before expecting or hoping for miracles in His name. She should try to be sure that it is for the glory of God rather than her own name that she is being zealous. Christ did not condemn the Pharisees because they lacked respect for the Law, for they did not. But He did condemn them because they perverted their respect for the Law's true end, the glory of God, to use the Law for their own glory.

The religious superior is always in danger of demanding obedience from the subjects primarily for the execution of her own plans rather than for their own sanctification. The indignation of the superior when disobeyed reveals this. It is the affront to her authority rather than to authority itself that hurts. If she were thinking objectively she would be anxious about the subject who disobeyed rather than about her flouted authority. The only injury under God is to the disobedient subject.

The superior overjealous of her authority does not so much develop obedience as conformity. The discerning person sees in these only the vaguest similarity. There will be a high degree of uniformity of action in the subjects of such a superior but only because they have abandoned almost all liberty in the hope of pleasing her for the sake of peace. Such a superior makes the fundamental mistake of forgetting her stewardship. She forgets that she cannot make the subject obey; she can only hope for obedience by imposing it properly and justly. She herself must first have the love and respect for God which her office demands, and be the first to demand obedience of herself. She should know that when obedience has to be enforced, it has come to mean little or nothing to the religious concerned. The vow of obedience means nothing because the virtue of obedience has never been acquired; the virtue can only be acquired by the free exercise of will, not by externally applied, irresistible pressure.

Because the average superior considers 90 percent of the matter of obedience to be the willing adaptability of the subject to the wishes or orders of the superior, a strange phenomenon is seen broadcast in religious life. Much more is expected of the untrained subject than of the supposedly well-trained superior. Even though it is said that the subjects need this because they are in a formative period of their lives, it is not really so. Certainly the best trained children do not come from the homes in which the parents are harder on the children than they are on themselves. Such children may appear to be well trained while their parents are within sight, but when they are free of parental observation they will take every liberty they have seen the parents take in their unguarded moments. Will religious subjects be noted for virtues they have not seen in their mentors?

A situation where criticism is not tolerated is unhealthy, as any businessman knows. There is a broad middle road between outlawing criticism by ruthless suppression and the anarchy that most insecure superiors fear so much. The superior who considers criticism censorious of herself can make it disappear, but this is a tragedy, for she is really the only one who needs to hear it. She ends up living in a fool's paradise, convinced there is no disharmony because she has driven it underground by her very unvirtuous resentment of it. Such a superior, lacking the virtues so essential in a good superior, is the first to resent her subjects seeking the advice of outsiders, even of their confessors and directors. She fears they are manifesting the shortcomings which her morbid resentment indicates she really knows she has. Second, she feels that their going to others makes it plain she herself does not have what her job demands. If she were wiser, humbler, she would know there is a natural bias against confiding in superiors, because the confidence then becomes a matter of obligation to the superior who cannot overlook it in making arrangements and appointments. This is one of the reasons superiors of men are not permitted to be confessors of their subjects. Then how could any religious go to a superior who obviously warrants little confidence? One would have to be a fool to do so. Where confidence is warranted it is generally given immediately. The superior who does not get it should look to herself rather than to her subjects for the reasons.

A child is born into its first school, not enrolled. Its mother is its teacher and there is no substitute for her. The first classroom is the home, and the effects of this school are seldom eradicated. Such is true of the formation of religious. If they are deprived of mothers with a deep love of God and a great sense of responsibility in the exercise of their authority, their loss is irreparable. The house built on sand must fall. So many parents, when they see their children go wrong, refuse to ask themselves how they failed in their duty. They loudly protest the ingratitude of the children when the children had precious little reason for gratitude. The same principle governs the relations of superiors to subjects in all things, but nowhere more certainly than in the building up of respect for authority which makes obedience an acceptable and profitable step in the process of holiness.

The superior has more than an obligation to inculcate obedience. Her subjects have offered their lives to God. These lives are God's. The superior must develop these people and their talents so that they are fruitful for God, and this development precludes any suggestion that the subjects can be turned into automatons or circus performers. The process demands reasonable, purposeful commands. The superior could not in conscience expect unreasonable commands to be obeyed. She herself would be the first to reprimand a subject for doing an unreasonable thing. But only the one commanded can be the judge of this. Even though she will be wrong sometimes she must be trained to make such judgments as part of her development. She must be corrected and learn to take the correction with the spirit of obedience. Instead of getting annoyed, superiors must understand that the spirit of obedience in subjects so acting is very high and their action is commendable.

No one actually knows another's mind; therefore the superior must always presume a subject to be acting reasonably unless the contrary is quite obvious. Any action having God's pleasure as its object should mirror the actions of the best superiors. This attitude is not prevalent, but until it is superiors will not be doing their work properly, and the virtue of obedience will never flourish as it should. Their job is to make the best of the material they have. Unless they think they are almighty God instead of His stewards, they will expect to make mistakes and wrong judgments, but this will not deter them from taking every worthwhile risk in going ahead. Not only will their judgment improve with experience but their subjects will be much more expansive, fruitful, and happy.

The second pole of obedience is the subject. To think of obedience from a single viewpoint is like thinking of a beginning without an end. The superior's obligation in obedience is to be a good religious herself, administering the things of God to the highest degree of her competence, rejecting any notion that she suddenly grew ten feet tall with her appointment. In her relations with her subjects their good must come first and foremost. The subject must undertake obedience with the idea of overcoming self and pleasing God, rather than men. It is no small thing to submit for life to one's equal or inferior. Only her constant vision of Christ before Pilate will make unrelenting obedience reasonable to the subject. Obedience for her must mean the opportunity of applying her talents to the greater good of her own soul, safeguarded by authority, and to the good of others under the aegis of the community she enters, responsible to the superiors duly elected or appointed to determine what is best for her. If these things are not present, obedience is a wasteful and unreasonable thing, detrimental to the religious herself and useless to the work of the Church. The

subject must therefore have no doubt about the obligation
to obey and be keen to understand the limitations within
which that obligation binds. She cannot serve God by safely
refusing to question the right to bind any more than she
can serve God by reserving to herself the right in each case
to decide whether it suits her or not to obey.

Utter servile response to the least ridiculous wish of a
capricious superior, while undertaken apparently out of blind
obedience, usually comes from lack of courage, the desire
to conform, or the wish to ingratiate oneself. But the con-
tinual qualification of circumstances under which she will
obey is not real obedience at all; it is a convenient fiction
which deceives only the religious herself, whose life will be
as whimsical as her obedience. The subject, then, has the
obligation to obey without question when she is obliged
and she must decide in her own conscience when that obligation is present, for she cannot, without betraying religious life
itself, forego the use of her intelligence and free will just
to make things easier for herself. Obedience is not expected
to make life easier, but to make a higher, better life possible.
This is not done by taking the easy way out and permitting
authority to overstep itself. Doing so removes the merit from
obedience.

Obedience is most important for the subject. Every trouble
of the religious can be traced back to pride, and this is the
object of the vow of obedience. By it pride the root of all
evil is controlled, and humility the basis of all virtue is
practiced. Superiors have no right to obedience in themselves, for they are nothing apart from their position. But
superiors do represent God and disobedience to them, like
disobedience to one's parents, is disobedience to God. That
must never be forgotten. There can never be sin unless God

is offended, but there can never be disobedience without offending God.

When through the grace of God a young girl decides to enter religion, it is because she sees in that life a way to love and serve God, thereby saving her soul. It does not occur to her that she might ever question the superiors who would be put over her. She is as docile as a human being can be, glowing with the sense of privilege in being a nun. However, being human, she overestimates her goodness; and her generosity has not until now been tried. She underestimates the penchant of all human beings to have their cake and eat it too. Passing through the anxiety of her novitiate, she is grateful for being called to vows, and hopes with God's grace to persevere until her finals. She is aware that she may not make the grade, may be asked to leave. Her trouble usually only begins after she has made her final vows, for then and only then does she really begin to be herself.

Religion does not change a woman's nature. Once they have finally given their lives to God, religious begin little by little to take them back under their own dominion. Whether it is done unconsciously or not, this is the beginning of the conflict with obedience. It would be the greatest help to religious if they could understand that this is the crucial period of their lives, and that it will generally be over the matter of obedience that the decisive battle will be fought. If without losing an iota of her zeal and ingenuity, drive and expansiveness, the religious can maintain her full willingness to obey, she will be all but matchless in her progress. How then can she do that?

First of all, every religious should have as much theological training as she can absorb. It is grossly unfair to withhold from religious, in favor of knowledge they need much less, the principles underlying their lives. There are still too many who think that knowledge is a threat to religious life; the life is too hard if one knows too much; one does better just going blindly on without thinking or asking too many questions. This is insulting to God. Obedience is unworthy of the name if one hardly knows what she is doing. There are others who hold that superiors should know more than their subjects, as if there were some trade secrets which could buttress their authority, making it unassailable, things which should not be revealed to the rank and file. Obedience is not accorded superiors by reason of their superior knowledge but by reason of their position, and it will certainly be assailed if they think it more secure amid ignorant subjects. The highest form of obedience is that given by a person who knows what she gives, why she gives it, and gives it freely. It is primarily because religious have not had this theological training that the crisis in authority has come to the fore. It is not obedience which is being questioned, but the extent of it.

Second, religious life must be rescued from the theology of minimums. In the practice of virtue one does not split hairs to determine how little one has to do to avoid sin. Virtue is growth, increase, bigness, and for obedience it is found in the gospel dimensions spelled out so clearly by Christ: "If a man take your coat, give him your cloak also; if he make you walk one mile with him, go another mile." A religious must not consider her responsibilities fulfilled when she has done to the letter what she has been asked or told to do by her superiors. She should be willing to do anything at all for anyone that is good or necessary, as long as she has no seriously conflicting responsibility. Without this spirit, obedience is but lip service. How often one hears the protest, "I would do anything in the world for her."

But when the protester is actually asked to do even a small thing, excuses are piled on excuses while her face betrays her relief at being able to nullify the generosity of her offering. So many are willing to do anything until it hurts, thanking God that it hurts so soon. Generosity truly begins when giving starts to hurt. Obedience really begins when it goes against the grain. With each act of obedience the virtue of obedience increases, and the letter killeth but the spirit quickeneth. Who aims at fulfilling the least required amount dies a thousand deaths with each command. Who develops the spirit of obedience to the utmost in all the things she is bound to, finds her spiritual life thriving. The truly docile religious hardly realizes what God does through her, nor is she aware of all the commands given her. Her reflexes are almost automatic. Refusal in her life is almost nonexistent.

When the good judgment of nuns is undeveloped, they are deprived of the training which makes real obedience possible. Many of the saints in their anxiety for the obedient spirit went to extremes in locating the limits of obedience. St. Ignatius insisted that the subject should be in the hands of the superior, "after the manner of a staff . . . after the manner of a corpse." This is an illustration, an analogy, perhaps very fitting for certain times and places or under certain conditions, but what superior wants a corpse on her hands? A corpse cannot merit. Actually to be a staff in the hands of a superior would imply that the superior always acted in a perfectly godly way. This should be her desire, but few would presume it to be a fact. No religious is ever permitted to abdicate her own conscience in favor of another's except, of course, the scrupulous, or those who through error have formed a false conscience and need the guidance of a competent person until they are fully responsible again. The *Lives of the Saints* are full of stories in which extravagant and unreasonable demands were made of subjects by superiors and great rewards lavished on them by God for compliance with these orders. But the demands were attributed to holy superiors who apparently sought to inculcate humility in their subjects. Holy superiors would be the first to know that God could be praised with nothing less than the truth and the best use of reason. They would be the first to discard the unreasonable and ridiculous as unworthy of God. A religious cannot be obliged to do the impossible, or anything conflicting with charity, the natural, divine, or ecclesiastical laws. Nor can a religious be required to take steps militating against her union with God or detrimental to her soul. For it is better to obey God than men. Regardless of the fact that this teaching exposes a religious to the danger of preferring her own mind to the orders of her superiors, it is a necessary danger against which she must be prepared and trained. The degree of sanctity she will reach, under the direct action of God, depends on this training, and her good will.

The test of good will is not difficult to make. Is a subject able and willing to speak calmly and truthfully about the grievances or criticisms she has? Is she as free with her criticism before her superior as she is before her fellow religious? To those who object that superiors are unwilling to listen or that punishment for criticism strikes like lightning might be addressed the questions: Have the superiors been given the benefit of the doubt? Are the objections warranted by experience? Has the superior actually rejected, out of hand, calm criticism properly made? Has the superior actually meted out unwarranted punishment for such efforts to be helpful? If a subject should never be condemned unfairly or unheard, it is even more necessary not to prejudge a superior. No subject of even slight good will would condemn a superior on the evidence of others. Properly trained, she weighs the criticism without being unduly influenced by it. Few superiors have it in them to resist the words and wisdom of the intelligent religious of good will. For truth is strangely penetrating and genuine good will disarming. What pass for truth too often in the small minds of men are their own stubbornly defended opinions, and what is considered good will is all too often their own deeply entrenched self-interest. This is always more apparent to the listening superior than to the protesting subject, for human nature is so blinded by pride and so tangled in ego. In all matters of obedience the rule permits and every good superior wants and expects representation.

In obedience, oversimplification reigns supreme. It is simply considered the work of the superior to command and the work of the subject to obey, and that ends that. Tragically, through failure to see her own responsibility, a religious can permit courtesy to become custom, and custom to become law, until there is little liberty left in her life even when tyranny has not yet begun to reign. For this reason the Church has tried to protect religious by ordering general chapters in which they are to express themselves and vote freely on various items by which they agree to obligate themselves. This surely is an answer to those who say that freedom to express one's mind lessens respect for authority. Where religious do not freely express themselves there is no respect for authority. The very best religious betray God when they have the chance to stand up and speak their minds and do not take it because of human respect. They insist on playing it safe and suffering any indignity rather than having their reputations questioned by standing up to protect their religious home against the destructive abuse of authority.

Religious life is the only life nuns know. It is the milieu in which they devote their time and efforts, body and soul, to their spouse, Christ. It is incomprehensible that any religious could be so detached about the condition of her home that she could let sloppiness or other conditions prevail which could not possibly be pleasing to her Spouse. Yet among the best religious are many who refuse to speak up, make recommendations, or propose changes in constitution or custom because they could not face the hostility of the lukewarm or the censoriousness of the administration. It has been so wrongly ingrained in them that criticism is incipient disobedience that they tolerate the loss of freedom rather than insist on every opportunity for the practice of virtue. The Child Christ, busy about His Father's business in the Temple, taught the venerable sages in the interest of His Father. In the same way, He cast the money changers from the Temple, cried out against the hypocrites who bound the people with unbearable burdens in the name of God. When such Phariseeism is allowed to creep into religious life, Christ is just as truly opposed as He was then. Nor can the individual escape her responsibility for this condition; denying its existence cannot make it go away. This failure of subjects to insure the proper application of obedience through legally constituted devices has led to the deterioration of religious life. The greatest responsibility lies at the door of the "good" religious, not the lax who have discredited themselves. By eliminating the "disobedient" spirit of criticism through silent general chapters, superiors have felt free to believe that there is no reason for it. The Communists now pride themselves on the spirit of self-criticism which used to be the mark of religious anxious for perfection. Religious on the other hand now look every place but in themselves for reason for the world's contempt. Only when obedience has been returned to its rightful place in religious life will young people vie with each other to submit themselves to an authority capable of providing for them a better way of life.

A nun appointed to vocation work prudently canvassed vocational directors, male and female, for their explanation of the dearth of vocations. The replies had remarkable unanimity, listing three main reasons for the shortage. First, the children of today are unwilling to make the sacrifices required by religious life. Second, the world is too seductive, its charms too available and irresistible to youth. Third, the parents are not doing their part in stimulating vocations, which come from happy homes where God plays a leading role.

A wise old priest, examining these replies, was shocked. He said, "I do not think these vocation directors could be more wrong than they are, on all three counts." From experience in three generations he believed the young people of today more willing to make sacrifices than any young people before them. Far from being seduced by the world, they are largely disgusted with it, and looking to their elders for direction and example that are not forthcoming. He also said that he thought parents were happier today than ever before to see their children in religion.

Today young people are subject to military service in peacetime. They are alert to the necessity of going any place in the world on a moment's notice, regardless of their personal wishes, to lose their lives in remote jungles for causes of which they may be doubtful. They expect a way of life, at least for some time, which used to be considered the lot of the martyr and the saint. Thousands of young people, without any particular religious convictions, are clamoring to join the peace corps, willing to spend some years of their precious youth undergoing intensive and demanding training, to carry learning and material help to the underdeveloped nations. Parents in the face of uncertain conditions in modern living are delighted if their children consider religious life, thus aspiring to the security of heaven. The young people are not impressed by the religious they meet. There is too much talk of virtue and too little evidence of it. Before giving up control over their lives young people want more assurance of the happiness available in religious life, promised but apparently not attained by very many. Religious life looks to them like a stock not producing enough dividend to make it a worthwhile investment.

Whenever youth has seen virtue flourishing, religious life has been irresistible and vocations have flourished. From the time of Christ through the catacombs and the Coliseum youth has risen to the challenge of heroism. From crusades to moon probes youth has been waiting to go. More than ever they are waiting today for the challenge to holiness. The honest religious must admit that far too much frailty has lurked under the mantles of religion. Hospitals once served the poor and neglected; now they are money-makers devouring the very souls of those dedicated to them. Schools were once provided by religious for the poor who would otherwise be uneducated; now Catholic schools are in competition with free government schools for all, few accepting students without high marks or the ability to pay. Religious whose specialty is God are teaching reading, writing, and arithmetic, while the laity teach catechism, and often do a better job of it. But very soon circumstances beyond the control of religious will change all this. Big institutions will be taken from their control and they will go out again to the sick and the poor, the tired and distressed. And they will have a host of helpers who want to give themselves rather than be devoured. A real challenge appeals to the frail seed of nobility in even the most depraved of men. Religion is not presenting that challenge, because its authority has been abused and the best of subjects have not objected.

Obedience cannot be legislated; it must be inspired. When Christ washed the feet of His Apostles He had to make sure they got the point. It has taken religious a long time to get the point of "he that is the greatest among you let him become the least." The title "sister servant" is indeed an empty one when her every whim is paramount with her subjects. Mother superior is an empty name for one whose maternal instinct is portrayed by tyrannical domination. Many good people are holding the garments of those slaying the prophets; it is to be hoped that some of them will end up as fortunately as Saul.

The greatest happiness reigns in the house where obedience is administered with love and a deep sense of responsibility. Such a house attracts subjects as honey attracts bees. To live in such a house is to live in the vestibule of heaven, where obedience is a privilege for the subjects who vie with one another in docility. Good parents consider themselves only baby-sitters for the best parent of all, God, whose image they hope to bring out in their children before their return to God. Could the religious father or mother be satisfied with less?

Not all parents are adequate or responsible, and the same can be expected of religious parents. Nuns teaching in schools often wonder how the children are as good as they are coming from the homes they have. They see children who have been neglected, abandoned, or even perverted by their parents, rising to unbelievable heights because through the grace of God they made up themselves for what the parents lacked. This has to be done often in religion where superiors are derelict in their duty. It must be done through a sense of obedience to God rather than men. So any discussion of obedience must end academically or with an open admission of the practical truth. There is on the one hand the superior holding for the respect due her position as God's representative, regardless of her irresponsible administration. There is on the other hand the subject rejecting the idea of respecting a superior because her administration in unworthy of the God she claims to represent. Both are equally wrong. There is also the superior knowing her inability to represent God worthily, accepting a job she cannot hope to fill, trusting in Him to help her with the limited resources she has, willing to admit her shortcomings and failings. And there is the subject interested only in obedience to God, regardless of who takes His place or what her qualifications are, never expecting of her superior something she is powerless to do, or demanding of her talents that she does not possess, only withholding complete conformity with her wishes in those things which are impossible for her or unworthy of the God to whom she vowed obedience. Thus we picture about as clearly as possible the boundaries of obedience. Within these boundaries every superior and religious must find and keep her place, living by her faith, on her hope, and through her charity.

Two delusions are to be avoided. The superior acting in the name of God with His blessing and authority might feel less obliged to be what she ought to be. The subject, turning over her own obligations to the superior's safekeeping, is liable to feel free from weighing the pros and cons of her actions. Nothing must permit the superior to forget her primary obligation to fulfill her duty to the very best of her ability, in a manner as worthy as possible of the God whose authority she claims. Nothing should permit the subject to make another responsible for the decisions that she alone can make and for which she will bear the full responsibility before God. The most tyrannical superior cannot place obligations on her which are not hers, nor can the most indulgent dispense her from those that are. To be a religious, whether subject or superior, is to profess a total dedication to God. It were better not to make it than to make it with reservations, for certainly only the fate of Ananias and Sapphira awaits the partially dedicated religious, withholding something for herself.

Happy is the house in which the superior never forgets the merciful God she serves, and where the subjects are mindful of the privilege that is theirs to serve God through obedience. Here the good superior seldom gives a command and the obedient subject seldom has to receive an order. The good superior is more interested in extending privileges to the religious and the good subject is more interested in fulfilling all her obligations. For the good superior recognizes that if her authority is questioned in a matter in which she is duly authorized, the religious subject has little respect for God; and the subject knows that if she has to be commanded she is negligent. The superior should never command something that could be legitimately questioned and the subject should never question something that could be legitimately commanded. Religious are too inclined to think of obedience as a vow instead of a virtue. Observance of the vow is measured in minimums, the practice of the virtue in maximums.

15. Community Life

THE Psalmist says, "Behold how good and how pleasant it is for brethren to dwell together in unity." And of course this Psalm has been quoted in praise of community life from its origin. Yet literally thousands of religious living in community would say "Phooey" to this. They do not discredit Sacred Scripture; they do not disbelieve it. They just consider that community life very frequently is not like that at all. It is not that it couldn't be; it is just that it is not. Before it ever will be, much soul-searching must be done by those who love religious life. Every religious must contribute every talent she has to offer if community life is to resound with the praise of God coming from undisguised, unfeigned happiness.

To the unwary any change appears to be improvement, but when something is added something is usually subtracted also. Real improvement drops the obsolete and useless while adding the good and helpful. The impetuous seeking relief from boredom never bring improvement. Only those anxious to conform in all good things can be trusted to make the changes that good things demand. Reason flowing out of goodness must prevail. It is the way of the young to forget that anything has been done in the past. Still the sluggish fossil who insists that what was good enough for her mother is good enough for her cannot be allowed to stand in the way of the young to whom the future belongs.

Community life is not for fish but people, and people need warmth. Children who come from a warm home and a loving family are happy. The disturbed child comes from a disturbed home. That same warmth should be found also in the religious home. Where it is missing the subjects are just as disturbed and unhappy as the children coming from the neglect and want surrounding the pleasure-bent selfish parents. There is the warm bond of blood in the family; there should be the warmer bond of grace and charity in the religious family. Where there is not, the community should be suppressed, for its life is marked by a coldness unworthy of the wicked witch of fairyland, let alone of Christian charity.

These communities can be marked by their community pride, often mistakenly called community loyalty. Their zeal is almost exclusively for the works of their own order, seldom for religious life, other orders, or the Church at large. Practicing a deplorable form of religious snobbery, they look upon other religious as competitors, to be ignored if possible, treated worse than schismatics if not. Their pride of order is accompanied by a fetish for anonymity. A book is published by "A Daughter of Solomon"; the phone is answered by "St. Romuald's Convent. Who is speaking please?"; a letter is sent to the students' parents signed "A Sister of Divine Praise." No one excels, no one is noticed; all individual personalities and talents are obscured as if to have the same lines in the face as in the material of the habit. But God help the nun who lets the order down!

This is hardly the way of the God who gave to each her very own fingerprints and who presents each with her very own graces. But so they think to remove pride from self to the order. Their only claim to fame is that they are privileged to be different from all others. Those entering the community must forget that this one was the daughter of the governor of the state or that one the sister of the president of such-and-such a corporation or the other one the aunt of some child movie star, because it would be a sin of pride to take pleasure in it. They must now restrict their pride to membership in the community as if their pride was less sinful because spread over so many individuals.

Religious in a warm community are sisters, and their superiors are truly mothers to them. They consider other religious to be sisters with themselves of Jesus Christ. This warmth of charity fosters individuality with the highest competition to serve each other and every other community in the Church. Even schismatics and heretics have their understanding pity and forgiveness. Good parents are ashamed of their children when their conduct toward the neighbors is reprehensible. Any community should be ashamed of its members when their behavior toward another community leaves anything to be desired. This is the way of the real Christian family.

The well-trained children from a large family live community life and have the least adjustment to make when they enter religion. They are used to sharing and getting along together. They accept discipline and doing without in favor of others. They are accustomed to assigned chores and being urged to fulfill responsibility. They vie with each other in relieving their parents of minor duties. They are the best evidence that community life begins in the home with proper parents. So religious community begins with proper superiors. The religious, inspired by selfless superiors who live close to God, have an advantage through no fault of theirs which can never be overestimated.

It is from the ultrastrict and overdisciplined homes of the world that the rebels pour forth. They are not better for feeling the lash of the tongue or the rod of correction on their backs. On the first opportunity they flee. The best homes are those in which the parents do the things which must be done and do not expect the impossible. A parent can give all the love and affection of which she is capable but she cannot command the love of the recalcitrant child. The return of parental love can only be made by the child itself. Parents sin who demand from the child the things that can only be freely given: love, gratitude, and respect. Regrettably, few parents understand that they have only one obligation, and that is with the help of God to be all they should be. The rest depends on the child. Anxiety to see in the child better behavior than their own leads parents to every abuse of authority. Unwilling to exercise the patient supervision of children during the formative years, some parents rule with an iron hand; others resort to bribery in default of duty; yet others in the face of scorn and indifference from their children give up any honest effort in their obligations which remain their obligations regardless of the response from the children.

These things can be just as truly said of the religious home. Where the home is ultrastrict there is the seed of revolt. The sisters are not better for the lash of the tongue or even the metaphorical rod of correction on their backs. They do not actually flee their home because of their vow, but they do withdraw to the cold refuge they build within themselves. They lock their hearts against their religious parents because they sense the wrong motivation for the discipline. They see the superiors eagerly taking credit for their good performance and disproportionately embarrassed by their poor performance, with little reference to or even interest in the divine displeasure. If these children do not fly the cloister they are hardly better than the lax religious who content themselves with minimal formal service to God while seeking their pleasures where they may, hoping to amend things sometime before the end.

In religion as elsewhere there is the retarded child. With more enlightenment, this fact becomes less a tragedy and more a grace. Parents in the world are immediately crushed by the retarded child. Their pride is dreadfully hurt. They feel guilt at having already betrayed the child by prenatal carelessness. Sometimes there are recriminations against a Providence which is all good and therefore can do only good. Seldom are the blessings accompanying the retarded child appreciated. First, it is all but a cure for unwarranted parental pride. Then, of course, it is a call to blind acceptance of something beyond the mother's comprehension. It is an opportunity to love someone who cannot repay that love by the knowing return which makes love easy and a pleasure. The other children in the family, far from rejecting that child or being ashamed of it, with the uncomplicated spontaneity of children born without prejudice, rally to its defense and protection. This develops in the other children the ability to forget themselves in the greater needs of others, and the objectivity required to distinguish a real treasure from a real tragedy.

The parents of the retarded religious child also react with shame that is out of proportion, as if by her failing the daughter went out of her way to embarrass the mother or the order, when in reality she was simply unable to cope with things or fulfill the vows for which she had been inadequately prepared. The retarded child of religious life has seen mothers who were so anxious to draw members into the community and yet unable or unwilling to train them properly for their life and work. It takes a real mother to recognize the retarded children of religious life as her very own, a cure for her pride and an appeal to give love as Christ gave it, without much hope or expectation of return. The heart of a real mother with a great capacity to think of others has a special love for those less endowed with grace. She offers their recalcitrance to God for her own sins and the sins of the community, which while more hidden are often more serious. All communities have these retarded children and they are as slow to admit it as worldly parents are to speak of their retarded children. The problem will be as slow in solution too, until the communities face facts, admit the numbers, and pool their resources to understand and treat the matter as intelligently as it can be treated.

As in the common life everywhere, it is the work of all who enjoy the privileges of community life to fulfill its obligations. One of the basic obligations is to preserve it; another is to enliven it; another, to reject anything detrimental to it. Too often superiors make it their exclusive right to determine what is good for community life, as if their subjects did not yet enjoy the use of reason or have the right to vote. Subjects accepting this state of affairs usually hope to absolve themselves from blame for its deterioration. It is for all superiors and subjects together, to examine their common life and do something about its failings.

The chapter of faults for instance, is a relic from other days. It was undoubtedly of tremendous value when people were less introspective or distracted and had perhaps a healthier, more objective outlook than they have today. Granted that the chapter was to deal with externals only, the exterior observance of formalities and rules, nevertheless none is so naïve as to deny that external observations flow from interior reverence for the will of God as expressed in the rules and constitutions. Therefore the distinction was purely academic. Some superiors rightly look on the chapter of faults as the only legitimate occasion for the competent superior to talk to her subjects with forthright honesty, but these superiors are regrettably few.

There may be some merit in scourging oneself, but there can be little in scourging another, even under the guise of godliness. In this day and age the chapter is a scourge to the just and a weapon to the unjust and all but useless in accomplishing whatever it was originally designed to do. It were better for all concerned if it were omitted once for all, or made voluntary for those who sincerely want the fruits which could be had from it. If it was intended to develop humility in religious, it has been a tremendous waste of time. Genuinely interested religious, after years of particular examen, fail to recognize predominant faults when almost anyone else could point them out with the greatest of ease. Nuns admit the greatest disappointment comes from the inability to come to grips with reality in themselves. Few people are ever helped until and unless they want help. This cannot be known when an exercise demands the participation of all regardless of their good will. It is hard enough to accept correction from those one loves and respects. Even the enlightenment of the soul by God passes unnoticed or rejected unless there is a very great love for Him. In a chapter of faults there is general foreboding lest a tender nerve be touched or that one is expected to make a charge for which in charity she can have little stomach. If there is real merit in the chapter of faults, it needs badly to be reworked and redesigned. If there is not, it should be dropped without further waste of time better employed in more profitable work.

For another thing, there is confusion in the schools today because of large enrollments and various systems of teaching. Learning would be completely hopeless if all students were put in the same class regardless of their qualifications, background, mentality, or interest. Yet this is done when meditation is made for all in public, spiritual reading in common, and when community prayers consist of a burst of licketysplit almost as meaningless as voodoo incantation. Meditation is personal; spiritual reading is too precious to be wasted on poor quality suitable for all; and changing the formal prayers every three or five years would at least demand greater attention to what is said. Certainly community prayers are not better for the number of years they have been neither modified, lengthened, nor abbreviated. Fewer prayers with more attention would be a good thing, though fewer could easily become none at all. Nor should attention be exacted beyond the commonly accepted time, which is about the span of a *Credo*. It must be remembered that prayer is union of the mind and heart with God and there is very little union when the body is on the prie-dieu but the mind has long ago retired. Routine can be as much evidence of a forgotten love as it can be proof of an enduring love, for routine's value depends a great deal on the motive behind it.

When sisters are assigned to special tasks or are operating under unusual stress or hurry, there should be a difference in the approach to their obligation of community prayers. Often the sisters should be dispensed from them altogether; at other times the prayers should be commuted to ten minutes before the Blessed Sacrament or some other sensible alternative. Some fear that this might lead to the arbitrary and even whimsical omission of prayers. This, of course, is true. But where there is the least degree of love of God there will be prayer because it is the only real communication between the soul and God. If after twenty years in religion, or even much less, the sisters have no taste for prayer or would neglect it entirely for their comfort, those twenty years or less have done very little for the sisters' union with God. The spiritual life does not depend on any routine but on the inherent love of God. It is a question whether more harm has come to religion and religious through the neglect of formal prayer than from the frantic urgency to fulfill the letter of the law when any calm, sensible person would realize there was no obligation. All that ensues from a panicky prayer-life is complacency and a false sense of being clear of all accrued debt to God.

It would be very interesting to know the number of nuns who look forward to recreation periods with mixed emotions because the tone and quality of conversation is determined by the mentality of the superior who dominates it, or because there will be nothing stimulating, provocative, or useful discussed. The nun today needs a grasp of current events. She should as a voting citizen have opinions which she has formed from mature reflection. Many Catholic institutions of learning suffer from the failure of teaching religious to delve into fields of correlated learning. If religious were restricted to the teaching of religion there might be somewhat less need of this broader knowledge, but when religious are responsible for scientific and humanist fields of learning there is no excuse for the poor quality of much of it. The quality can be traced to the conviction of small minds that thinking about these things is detrimental to interior quiet and spiritual growth. Yet religious are the first to claim that all knowledge must lead to God. Silence is sacred in religious life only because it helps to greater awareness of God's presence in the soul. But silence can also be due to a mental blank, a sort of mental Nirvana in which nothing goes on. This silence renders a religious almost incapable of intelligent conversation of any kind, or the simplest useful discussion.

There are many times when silence is required by rule but charity demands that words be spoken. True, there is provision in most rules for this, but let any religious use her own judgment to determine what is or is not charity and she will be roundly rebuked in public or accused at the chapter of faults. Silence must be respected, for in the silence of one's soul God is best heard. Silence is observed in the chapel because the Divine Presence is there. But to deny that almighty God is as truly present, albeit in a different manner, in the midst of two or more engaged in worthy conversation is heresy.

A happy home is known by the freedom of those blessed with the privilege of living in it. What mother coming in from shopping does not rejoice that she can sit in a comfortable chair, drop her shoes from her tired feet, and relax? This freedom should be felt in convents, even though it is hardly to be recommended that the sisters go around in their bare feet. One time when this freedom to relax should be especially felt is during the periods of recreation. And this is more necessary in the complicated twentieth century. Few nuns today are not living double lives, teaching while still working on their university degrees, or acting as part-time laboratory technicians while floor supervising. Their recreation should afford the greatest relaxation. Therefore, when it becomes a bore or a tedious devotion to Scrabble or the week's mending, regardless of personal tastes and inclinations, it is a penance rather than a recreation. As much free time should be given the sisters as is compatible with their vocation, and as much choice of recreational hobbies should be available as will accomplish the purpose of a genuine recreation. Why should it be compulsory to sit around a big table feigning attention to inanities and trivialities (which certainly no priest would put up with), when more interesting and entertaining activities could contribute to the happiness of the community and the individuals in it? Is it because someone might feel excluded or hurt? Or must recreation be on the lowest mental level in the community and satisfy only neurotic self-pitiers who are unable or unwilling to make any contribution to the common good or to take advantage of the silent leisure they could otherwise be permitted? This silence could be enjoyed immensely by many who would delight in reading a good book or listening to good music.

Communities are making a more serious effort to have vacations almost devoid of rule and the rigors of silence, so that from the change in routine the sisters can return to religious life more refreshed. Yet some religious look upon such things as unwarranted interruptions of a routine sanctified by time if not by spiritual progress. The older folks who, like the blind, are confused by the furniture being moved from one corner of their lives to the other need not be involved in such plans. Not all religious are "blind" and certainly at times almost any change is refreshing.

The religious habit is being assailed from all sides, to the understandable chagrin of many nuns who are accustomed to it and have no complaint. But the Holy Father was not wasting his time when he appealed for serious changes in it. At least he thought he was not, even though his appeal was all but in vain. Some few small changes were grudgingly made. Like it or not, the automobile licensing bureau has had more influence on the nuns and their habits than did the Holy Father. It simply would not, in fact, in conscience could not, grant licenses to communities wearing headgear which would disqualify a horse from pulling a milk truck through the city streets. It is not an easy thing to modify religious habits, but neither is it impossible. Certainly, even though many of the leading designers of women's clothes are men, it is a job for women; but let them get on with it. If they delay too long the communists will do it it fast enough in a way more radical than any yet suggested. Those responsible for the changes want to be sure that they will be for the best, that all will be pleased. They don't want to go to endless expense for hundreds or thousands of sisters only to find in a year or two the changes were really no improvement. But there is no necessity for being final in the changes, or insisting that whole communities change at once when small pilot groups could try out various changes over a given period of time.

Why could not the sisters have a habit for inside the convent and a suitable dress for outside, as male religious in America do? A reasonable length of time should be set aside by every community at the end of which a change based on modesty, economy, utility, and grace could be made without delay. Few nuns realize that the same intransigence they show in relation to the habit is also shown in relation to many of the changes that need to be made in their hearts and spiritual lives if they are ever to be worthy spouses of

Christ. The nuns were rightly amused at the designers of beautiful creations, inspired by the Pope's request, who drew sketches of possible habits which would make any airline hostess the envy of her competitors. The nuns knew that many of their number resembled the airplane more closely than the hostess. But youthful reconciliation to a monstrous habit which may have grown into an attachment does not excuse the nuns from doing something about it. What was good enough for Catherine of Siena is *not* good enough for Mary McGonigle of Paducah, Kentucky.

Apart from economy and uniformity, the underlying reason for the religious habit is the modesty it represents. But the religious bathing suit puts the challenge of modesty in its clearest terms. Until recently many communities did not permit the nuns to go swimming. However, with the advent of girls into religion who were raised in the world of summer vacations, beaches, and the freedom of abbreviated dress for comfort and for sports, without ever seriously considering that their modesty suffered any real setback through this, more and more communities have permitted their nuns to go bathing. Some of the suits have been a cross between a modern bathing suit and a coat of armor. It never dawned on those communities sticking to the archaic suits and shrouds of the early 1900's that if they had intended drawing the attention of the world to themselves they could hardly have been more successful than they were by appearing thus clad on the beaches where most people thought a past-century movie was being shot. Nor did it dawn on them that it were better not to go swimming publicly than to make such a spectacle of themselves and religion. Still others went to the other extreme and wore almost anything that could be called a bathing suit, many of which were anything but modest. It suddenly dawned on the thinking nun why some of them had no inherent sense of modesty. The habit had eliminated any necessity for thinking of modesty or adverting to propriety of dress in any way. When a good woman buys a dress she must ask herself if it is modest, avoiding what is archaic and too daring at the same time. The modest is that which does not attract undue attention. A nun bathing in a shroud attracts far more attention than any woman in a modest bathing suit, and it is more provocative because it is also known that she is a nun. Few unessential things have so underlined the poor judgment of nuns as their choice of bathing suits, unless it is the swimming pools in their institutions which are good enough for Catholic girls but unfit for use by nuns themselves. They do not violate modesty for the best of girls, just for the best of women.

Every religious community should appreciate the differences in people, and once for all desist from treating nuns as identical, making them all fit the same mold. Each comes to God with different gifts to offer for the good of the community which should rejoice in the variety. Why should adults be lined up and marched to church as if they were inmates of some orphanage of the 1800's? Many pastors groan in long-suffering — granted that they groan easily — when the sisters parade into church five minutes late for a second Mass on Sunday morning to fill pews reserved for them. Most of the sisters were lined up in time but could not leave the convent without the superior who had a penchant for being late. If some of the nuns could get there early or stay a little later after Mass they could meet many of the parents of the children they teach, with good effect on all. There are many times and places in the apostolate where more freedom for the nuns would be fruitful without destroying or even damaging their spirituality. Nuns in the foreign missions are almost useless without this freedom and they find life in the convents at home almost intolerable after it. There is little time in the mission field to worry about whether being outstanding for some specialty endangers a nun's humility or represents an occasion of sin to her. She must throw herself into the work with more abandon and generosity; conformity cannot receive her total consideration.

Economy is a necessary part of religious life from the point of view of poverty, yet it has become the great dictator in many community decisions. Nuns who entered religious life for their own salvation and the souls of others find themselves lavishing all their attention on a comptometer in the hospital office, the kitchen stove, or an algebra class. Yet none of these things has much direct relationship to religion or religious life. There was a day when hospitals, schools, orphanages, and other works depended for their very existence on the charity of nuns. But that day is nearly gone. The government supplies hospitals, schools, children's homes, and most of the agencies of welfare. True, the inspiring work of selfless nuns has done a lot to bring this about. But the day is at hand when the survival of the Church as a public influence will depend on the service of nuns in strictly religious work. Then their singleness of purpose may be restored and greater happiness return to their cloister home. Nuns' lives are wasted in occupations which seculars can do better while many jobs are undone because they lack people devoted enough to undertake them.

The one feature of community life which requires the immediate attention of experts is its furnishings. For the real furniture of the religious community is not the prie-dieu of the nun, the desk she works at, the table she eats from, or the chair on which she rests. The real furniture of the community is the material of the spiritual life, leading to a fuller life and greater union with Almighty God. Needless to say, the nun has the grace of God and the sacraments as has every Catholic, but she needs music, literature, art, drama, and many other things which give her inspiration to thought and incentive to action. There should be no community in the Church without its skilled team of nuns devoted to contributing directly and exclusively to the spiritual life of the Church. Why should the quality of Catholic literature remain so bad? The amount of it so small? Why should the masters of the middle ages be the only source of pride when the talents for better work and extraordinary materials are more abundant and available today? Why should the choice of hymns be restricted to a few worn-out tunes in honor of God when the world's composers of popular music and love ballads record new songs by the thousands annually? Why should so many illiterates, who could be brought to God through doctrine put to music, remain dependent on books they cannot read and words they cannot understand, despite an inborn love for music and a memory keen for sounds that please? Thousands of toys and games are designed to attract and entertain young people with appetites whetted for space travel and science, when without a doubt the most fundamental and interesting search in the world is the search for God and the joy and happiness which never passes. These are the very challenges for which the religious is especially prepared. They are the furnishings of her home. The nun interested in her home and way of life should be avid to make it more beautiful and her job more enjoyable and intriguing. The world has multiplied labor-saving devices to accomplish more chores with less effort; the village well has been piped to the house, electricity has turned night into day, central heating has banished the wood pile and brought summer to the igloo. Yet thousands of dedicated religious have contributed nothing to the means of closer union with God and happier lives; have made no effort to match the development of science in every other field. This is the great failure of community life which many have no time to think about because they are busy about less essential things than God Himself.

Few young couples doubt their marriage will be a happy one, or that their home will enjoy warmth, or that their children will be well adjusted and happy. But mature religious know how few are the really happy homes. It should be no surprise to nuns that their community life suffers the same defects as other institutions or organizations, for all are made up of people with every human weakness. While the sensible person accepts this fact she is not absolved from the effort to make a happy home or a joyous community life. God has His own way of adding to honest effort and placing those who administer five cities well, in charge of yet another ten. The God who made the world from nothing has a little more to work on to create something from the good will of even a few religious. Sodom and Gomorrah could have been saved by ten just; five loaves and two fishes fed five thousand. It is so unnecessary to say "Phooey" to the Psalmist, when a little effort by a few can bring so much help from God who inspired the Psalmist to say, "*Quam bonum et quam jucundum habitare fratres in unum.*"

16. Prayer

To DISCUSS religious life without discussing prayer is not to discuss religious life at all. Where there is no prayer there is no religious life. The interior life of the nun who does not pray is like the life of the man who does not eat. Life is there at the start, but it can only wither and die.

What then is prayer? It is the union of a human being with God. It is the supreme act of human existence on earth, a foretaste of the eternal union of heaven. It is the epitome of religious living. It has been called the raising of the mind and heart to God; an elevation of the soul to God; or, as St. Augustine put it, the soul's affectionate quest for God. Nowhere is the tongue of man more crippled than in trying to define prayer, for it is all these things and more, all these things and yet none of them. For generations the word "elevation" or "raising" and the metaphorical acceptance of the location of God's home in heaven as "up" had real significance. But with the present knowledge of space and the infinite dimensions of the universe, "up" is a mysterious word. Where is "up"? And why should one raise her mind to God when He is in the depths of her own soul? There is no answer to these questions. Prayer remains communication between the human being and God.

There is a poignant sadness in comparing the calm joy

of the simple, holy soul so easily communicating with God in prayer and the frantic effort of the scientist working to communicate with his fellowman. Man has so much to say to God and so little to his fellowman. Yet modern communications between men have taken eons of time, generations of thought, and mountains of money, while communication with God in prayer requires no time, no work, no cost.

Prayer is everything from the quiet, intense repetition of the Our Father as spelled out by our Lord, to the ineffable, ecstatic union of the soul with God in which, without sensing or understanding it, the soul knows beyond doubt or delusion what the truest love is.

Many nuns speak of their "prayer-life" as if it were a phase of living distinct from their essential life, a sort of heavier garment to be picked up or discarded at whim, or depending on the climate of need. Christ corrected this notion when He said to pray always. St. Paul commanded the Christians to pray without ceasing. Therefore Christian life is the life of prayer. They are the same. Anything the nun does is prayer unless she perverts her life by infidelity. The spiritual life, the pursuit of holiness, the following of Christ, prayer are all one and the same thing. There should therefore be less preoccupation with words and more actual prayer.

Reporting one's life history to God is not prayer. Our Lord spoke of the Pharisee and the Publican going up to the Temple to pray. The Pharisee's intention was completely vitiated by his effrontery in using the time to inform God of something He was more aware of than the Pharisee, and which had nothing whatever to do with prayer. If he thought he was praying he was certainly deluded. Religious are deluded when in prayer they thank God for any reason whatever that they are not like their fellowmen, even the Pharisee.

And religious do often thank God they are not like the Pharisee. Recall the thought-provoking picture of Christ standing, staff in hand, at the door of a house, knocking. The words, "Behold I stand at the door and knock," are very moving as nuns consider the unwillingness of the world, and even of many religious, to open their hearts to Christ. Yet the stunning thing is that few, reading the words or contemplating the picture of the rejection of Christ, think to apply the scene to themselves rather than to their neighbor. So distracted are they by the closed doors of the neighbors, they do not even hear the knock on their own door. By their personal rejection of Christ they are missing the whole point. They reject Christ because they have no communication with God, no prayer in their lives. Prayer has little interest for one with greater interests than God.

There was a nun who spent most of her religious life working among the old men of a home. She had served them faithfully and enjoyed their gratitude. Of course the years caught up with her. The weight of her chores was too much for her diminishing strength. She was not unhappy in what she was doing, just unequal to continuing alone. In answer to her complaints, her expressed hopes and desires, a young sister was appointed to help her and learn the routine of the work. The young sister was not there very long before it became quite obvious that the old men had much more interest in her than in the older nun. Surely if the old nun had known half as much about old men as she thought she did, this would have been no surprise to her. However, how could she know the old men when she did not even know herself? She deeply resented her abandonment by the group she had served for so long, so faithfully, for the more gracious smile and unwrinkled face of her junior in religion. Had she prayed better, had her work been primarily for Christ, she would not have had to learn so harshly that it was to the old men she gave her life rather than to Christ. If she had been working for Christ, despite some emotional pangs, she would have rejoiced at younger hands, quicker steps, and stronger muscles doing what had to be done for the aged. It is tragic to see this woman retired in bitterness and resentment when she might have been happy. After so many arduous years of consuming tasks she could now have more time to spend with Christ in prayer, making ready for the days of eternal youth and full happiness. Had her interest been in Christ, her life would have been spent in winning souls to Him rather than to herself. This active form of prayer would have kept her from ending her days depressed by the petty faithlessness of others, oblivious of her own faithlessness to Christ from the beginning.

Prayer should not be confused with daydreaming. The vocally talented nun who envisions herself singing the lead in an opera or giving a concert in Carnegie Hall is obviously daydreaming. But so is the nun who sees herself slaving in the jungles of Africa for the lepers or languishing in a communist prison. The material of the dream does not determine whether or not it is prayer. Given the opportunity, the one daydreamer would learn that she could suffer about as well as the other could sing. But those who daydream without noticing it seldom pray without noticing it. And those who notice they are praying are not praying at all. The reason prayerful souls seldom daydream without noticing it is that they have an interior sensitivity to God which recalls them when they forget Him. The bricklayer lays bricks without too much awareness of what he is doing because he is good at his task, but he does not pick up a hammer instead of a trowel without noticing it.

The nun who keeps the rule has been extolled without reserve, but she is not necessarily a woman of prayer. She is a well-trained woman exteriorly, but she does not necessarily have much interior union with God. The letter of the law means so much more to her than the spirit. The exterior training has not made itself felt in her interior life. One can have exterior conformity to a very high degree without interior union, for the former pleases oneself while the latter pleases God. The first fruit of prayer is the service of God, for the prayerful nun has no other interest. When the rule is kept because of union with God the nun is a prayerful woman, but she is also a free woman. The prayerful nun is not marked by unusual periods of time spent alone before the Blessed Sacrament or sequestered from her companions, even though the prayerful soul loves solitude. The union of the prayerful soul with God, even when in the substantial presence of Christ in the Blessed Sacrament, reminds her that He is everywhere, deep in her own soul, as well as in the souls of her sisters.

The signs of prayerfulness in an individual are more obvious to those around her than to herself, for she has no overwhelming interest in herself. She is notably selfless; her investment is in God's presence around her, in her work, in her associates, and in her beneficiaries. She loves truth, goodness, and beauty and sees them all around her, without lacking realism. She has an immediate awareness of untruth in her own life. She is as sensitive to a lie as her skin is to sandpaper. She makes no frantic effort of please herself, but every quiet effort is to please God. For her, prayer is growth in holiness, closing the distance between her soul and God, the thing she wants above all else. There is in her little interest in things not directly connected with God. Her love for others is so good and true because it stems from her love for God. Because of the identity of her will with God's, given the opportunity she is the one who would actually die for them. His evaluation of souls is hers to the degree of her capacity, the measure of her selflessness. Her love of God precludes evil; for it is impossible to be united with God in prayer and turned away from Him by sin at the same time.

The absence of direction is another indication of the prayerful nun. One treats directly with God in prayer, and the more direct the contact with God the less is the need of indirect contact, the less need of direction. But this does not leave the prayerful soul the least contemptuous of direction. Few are more aware than she of the tendency of the wishful thinker to consider her lack of direction as a sign of her holiness. Hers is not the logic of the homemade saint. She esteems spiritual guidance but she knows that if it is needed it will be available. When it is available she is the first to take it. She is never too proud to eat of the crumbs that fall from the Master's table, nor does anyone know better than she that they are crumbs. But she looks to God in prayer and gets the help He knows she needs. Prayer is after all a community of interest with God, and it shows as clearly as the community of interest between husband and wife. God does direct the soul united with Him in prayer and He does provide adequately for her. It is never His intention that a spiritual director come between Him and His spouse. The good director knows his job is to make himself superfluous as soon as possible. He never replaces

Christ; Christ never leaves the soul an orphan.

The state of the prayerful religious can no more be hidden than can a light on a lampstand or a city on a hill. Iron cannot rest in fire without absorbing heat; neither can a soul be immersed in God without being identified with Him. The heat of the iron depends on its absorbent qualities, after the heat of the fire itself; if the heat is intense enough it consumes the iron. If the union of the soul with God is intense enough the soul is consumed by God. It exists only in Him and for Him. This union is plainly seen by those not too blinded by jealousy and envy. They cannot think of such people without at the same time being mindful of God. It is objected, "You are still dealing with human nature; you still have to contend with human frailty." True enough, but the union with God made possible through the grace won by Christ's death on the cross was precisely to take care of human nature. Reborn by grace, made a child of God, heir to the kingdom of heaven, the nun through grace can rise above purely human nature. If this were not the case how could she be encouraged to take vows impossible for her to keep? Can the man unable to rise above himself give up the riches of the world, eliminate sexual satisfaction for his lifetime, or submit himself for life to another? The prayerful religious does this.

The skill of the artist is manifested by the movements of the brush in his hand. The greatness of the religious comes from her union with God, achieved through prayer. Prayer moves the soul to virtue; virtue is God at work through the soul. Prayer makes the soul the instrument of God in the world. It attaches the soul to God as the instrument is attached to the hand of the artist, purposeful, useful to the degree of its attachment and docility in God's hands.

It has already been said that the nun without prayer is like the man without food. However, just as many men eat badly, many nuns pray badly. This mistake is often compounded by concluding that God will compensate for it by accepting the motive for the deed, making it immaterial whether one prays badly or well, as long as the intention is not to pray badly. Surely there is more to praying well than this would indicate. There must be some objective value to praying well. How then does one pray well?

First of all, the descriptive terminology of prayer is not important. The prayer of quiet, vocal prayer, mental prayer, affective prayer, public or private prayer, the prayer of impetration, thanksgiving, reparation, or adoration — the kind of prayer it is means little or nothing in itself. It is easy to get lost in the labels and forget all about praying. Second, concern about self, not prayer, is evidenced by the primary interest of many in what state of prayer they may be. They are eager to know whether they enjoy the prayer of quiet or the state of affective prayer. They are easily led into thinking they enjoy either of these because they want to believe they do, or because some presumptuous soul tells them in a burst of enthusiasm that they may be in such a state. If the person herself cannot be sure there are few if any others who can be. A very wise, learned, and holy director might be able to tell her with some assurance of being right, but such a one if available would be very reticent about giving any such assurance. So rare are such directors that any nun meeting one in her whole lifetime would be fortunate indeed. At any rate, prayer is interest in God and one's aptitude for it is in inverse proportion to interest in oneself.

Granting these things, how can a soul set about praying well? Christ clearly outlined the answer when He replied to this very question by the Apostles. He gave all men for all time the Our Father. Its introduction was evidence enough of its divine origin. There was the salutation or address, the appreciation of God's dignity, the express desire for His dominion over all. These are the basic things in any prayer. No prayer is worth uttering unless it is with the hope that God will do as He knows best. In other words, it must always be the desire of the one praying that God's will be done. Although it is inconceivable to any reasonable, believing person, the commonest reason for the inefficacy of prayer is the tendency of people to tell God not only what they want, but just how and in what circumstances He is to give it to them. Be it ever so ludicrous in theory, it is ever so common in practice for the soul to presume in prayer to direct God. Religious who think they are exempt from this propensity deceive themselves. There is only one reason for the prayers of religious to remain unanswered, and that is that they expect them answered in the way they wish, as if God had no better judgment than they. No prayer rises much above the low level of superstition that is addressed to a power which could be influenced to support a human judgment with so little objectivity. To pray to God is to know that He is God, that He never makes mistakes, and that He can be the author of nothing but good. This certainly demands the abandonment of all one's own opinions, desires, and convictions to God. It does not rob the soul of convictions; it simply makes more certain that the soul's convictions come from God.

But the Our Father is more than words. It is a recipe for living. One is not just to say, "Our Father who art in heaven . . ." One is to walk through life in its darkest moments putting one's foot confidently down on an earth set there as surely by one's father as the city streets were laid by the municipality. And so with every other article of the prayer. It is to be lived, every day, all day, all the days of one's life. This is done by the religious who really prays well.

Since they are creatures of body and soul, walking in time and space, living by weights and measures, the prayer of human beings cannot be something only of the spirit, begun at a nudge from the Holy Ghost. Time must be given to prayer. But it is the man not the prayer that needs the time. If the religious has the time and does not give it to prayer, there is no real union with God, no real will to pray. But where there is no time for formal prayer as such she must not fail to understand that her life is her prayer, and that communion with God in her responsibilities, tasks, or conditions is not only possible but inevitable when she loves God. The soul loving God could not go through a day without thinking of Him. No day is so hectic or task so absorbing that the mind of the lover forgets the beloved.

Although no amount of external activity can interrupt the soul's union with God, no soul with leisure should let it pass without some recourse to formal prayer and the effort to be alone with God. Certainly any soul with time to be lonely has leisure. The religious who is lonely is not giving her leisure time to God. The nun should not expect to feel the fruitfulness of the time given to God; she should only realize that she could not love God and refuse or neglect to give it. But it is not the way of God to reward the prayerful person by letting her fall victim of her own satisfaction. He does reward her by letting her see herself more clearly, and this explains her disgust, her sense of hopelessness, and the intolerance of her own best efforts. And this is good because it brings her to the conviction that only one thing makes despair unreasonable: the tremendously clear understanding that God loves her not because of her goodness but because of His goodness. This goodness alone makes despair the grossest insult to God, because the despairing finds no love in the God who is Love Itself. This is the soul who belongs to the class in pseudo sanctity. She loves the discussion of prayer rather than prayer itself, and it is usually discussed to impress her hearers. She loves to discuss the heights and depths of prayer without ever thinking of soaring to God to seek Him in the depths of solitude, by prayer.

Prayer is essentially communication which is always better and clearer for the removal of all extraneous factors and material impediments. The elimination of these obstacles will always be taken care of by God if the soul will permit it. For those consumed with the struggle to be prayerful perhaps the only thing to say is that there is nothing much worse than being with a person who feels she must make conversation, who has to empty her own little garbage can of troubles upon anyone who will listen. After all, God does read the secrets of the heart. If the soul aspires to love God, He knows it. But can she ever find that out if she never stops to listen, or never gives her Companion credit for the intelligence to understand her without examining the blueprints of every little detail of her dull and uninteresting life? How could anyone's life be anything but dull when she is convinced she has more to tell God than she has to learn from Him?

17. Sin and Penance

THERE is a great deal involved in sin — such a small word for such a big thing. It is a disaster all the harder to understand because it is self-inflicted. Almost any calamity is more easily understood. Wars, atomic bombings, famines, fires, floods, earthquakes, tidal waves are all disasters which can be and are accepted with various degrees of resignation. In the disaster called sin no victim can blame anyone but himself. The things lost by sin are deliberately lost, they are thrown away. The greatest of those things is eternal happiness; it is thrown away forever by final impenitence.

Death was a disaster for man but God provided a remedy. Sin is eternal death and for that too God has provided a remedy. He established the sacrament of penance for the forgiveness of sins. If life was a great gift to man, that which restores lost life is the next greatest gift. The forgiveness of sin is very important to the religious for it can, among other things, restore lost life to her.

There can never be a question about the willingness of God to forgive sin. David was inspired by God to say, "A contrite and humble heart Thou shalt not despise." Isaias said, "If your sins be as scarlet they shall be made white as snow; and if they shall be red as crimson they shall be white as wool." It has always been the privilege of the sinner to return to God as the Prodigal Son returned to his father, not because he deserved forgiveness but because he would be forgiven. The puzzling thing about the tribunal of penance is that it enables men to seek forgiveness through men. "Who has known the mind of the Lord or who has been His counselor?" God has His own reasons for what He does. But one might conjecture that, since sin comes through pride, it is forgiven through humility. Seeking pardon from God through one's fellowman is humiliating, if nothing else. Even the holiest of people must do this much. Strangely enough, holy people do not have nearly as much trouble seeking forgiveness through men as do those who would like to believe they are holy, and would like everyone else to believe it too. The religious who has trouble with confession is usually one of these, or, even worse, one whose burden of guilt is so great that she cannot take God at His word.

The sacrament has much to offer religious if it is correctly understood and used. But it can be an ordeal for many of the best and purest women in the world. It can be a tribunal of anxiety rather than liberation to joy; a rack on which souls are stretched and torn rather than an inn where oil and wine are poured into wounds; a terminal from which burdens are carried away rather than a haven where cares are set down. For yet others this sacrament designed to make them better is wasted because they think they are good enough as they are.

Much of the trouble religious have with confession comes from the failure to distinguish between sorrow for sin and shame. These are more concerned about what their neighbor thinks than about what God knows. Sorrow for sin is exceedingly important. Shame is not. Sin in her life should be no surprise to any human being. It is said, even a just man falls seven times a day. Sorrow is the reaction of the sinful soul to her God; shame is her reaction before her neighbor. The former reveals her humility; the latter her pride. Sometimes it is hard to tell the difference. A nun slapping a passerby in the face on a public thoroughfare would have no trouble finding material for confession. However the enormity of her action would be plain more because of the locale in which it took place than because of the action itself. Would she go to confession because of her sin or her shame? How many religious go to confession regularly with a sense of sinfulness? How many actually have a struggle to find something to tell, even exaggerating a little to provide material for absolution? Because the sacrament is not only to forgive sin but to maintain in the penitent such a sense of sin that it will be avoided when possible, routine confessions without serious matter can lessen the esteem for confession and minimize its value. Christ, addressing Himself to the paralytic, first took care of the man's big trouble, his sins. But the Pharisees would only be impressed with the healing of his physical ills.

If a sister suffered from some gross illness from which she was suddenly and mysteriously cured, the word of this would go through the convent quickly, and through the whole community. In fact with some superiority and all "due humility" the other communities of the city or state would soon hear about it. Yet the truth of the matter is that each nun in the community, every week, is the recipient of a greater favor than this without any sense of the extraordinary. She goes to confession and has her sins forgiven. Because this thing has become routine its real significance passes almost unnoticed. It seems that curing of the body of a religious commands even more respect than the curing of a soul; matter eclipses spirit even where it should not. Little sins are taken care of regularly, with less and less attention given them, until they almost pass unnoticed. Where there is this condition God has little alternative but to let the soul stumble from one sin to another until she remembers what manner of woman she is. Being made holy, she would take it all for granted and believe she had never really been anything else. Thus the sacrament would waste one of its greatest graces, the power to make her holy.

Confession becomes an ordeal generally because of some folly in the field of purity, which for some reason seems to evoke more shame in the heart of religious than idolatry. The folly usually lies in the failure to distinguish between temptation and sin. Through negligent training in purity, understanding of the lot of every woman is poor. Many do not differentiate between what is to be expected, endured, and ignored, and what is to be repented of, confessed, and forgiven. Religious should know that this comes from looking at the matter of sin through the distorted eyes of the offender rather than through the forgiving mind of God.

Humility is the foundation of the spiritual life; pride is the main obstacle. And pride originating in the misfortunes of youth relating to purity is a common impediment to spiritual progress. Many religious have had some fairly normal experiences of childhood, which they think uniquely their own, in which through curiosity on their own part or that of their companions they explored some of the secrets of the human body. It is evident to them that this was in itself wrong. However, the enormity of what was done or could have happened became apparent only later on in life through enlightenment or instruction of some kind. Often the realization of the enormity came not so much from what happened as from speculation about what others might think if they only knew. This has little to do with sin but much to do with pride and the nun can let herself be blackmailed by her pride into long-lasting and tormenting misery which only the devil could enjoy. As it continues the problem continues, vague and unimportant at the time of confession, only to erupt afterward. The religious is tempted to believe some or all of her confessions have been bad, even though her common sense should tell her better. The torment and turmoil make tranquillity of soul as impossible as indifference to seasickness. This poor soul joins the corps going to one annual retreat after the other dreading the accusing finger of hypocrisy and insincerity. She almost always returns from the retreat without the assurance craved. She is never sure in her mind that the confessor understood what she was saying. Yet her life is tragic only in that her sorrows are self-inflicted.

What should such a religious do? The police are giving the answer day after day to the victims of blackmail. Refuse to be blackmailed. The victim of blackmail never finishes paying. She is a victim of her pride and fear. She should face what bothers her and be as simple, direct, and decisive as possible in dealing with it. How small the courage needed to admit she is wrong and say she is sorry, compared to the agony of carrying a straw load she believes is iron. No nun looking at her crucifix could doubt that her trouble is not in facing Christ but in facing herself. God seems to forgive so much faster than she forgives herself. Many, many nuns share this experience.

The enormity of a sin does not make it harder for God to forgive. The sorrow God asks is for the offense not the pleasure involved in the sin. One cannot be sorry for pleasure but one can be sorry for sin. A woman cannot regret wearing a mink coat but she can regret stealing the money to buy it. Nor does the confessor have to understand every grimy little detail of what was done or experienced. He need only know the kind of sin that was committed. She must remember that all she has heard about sins of impurity being mortal does not change the fact that with children they seldom are because of defective knowledge and will. Few mortal sins of impurity can be committed before the age of puberty. What was done was usually more from curiosity than malice and this is venial at worst. But the thing that all religious should understand is that the act of humility involved in facing self and clearing up the matter is usually the door opening to a unity with God not attainable by the proud. The stupidity of letting anything whatever come between herself and God is only really plain when seen from the other side of the low gate of humble sorrow. The soul which loves God will eventually refuse to tolerate anything that could hold her back from Him.

The tendency to think of things as black or white rather than one of many shades of gray leads people to think of themselves as either innocent or guilty of sin. How often one hears, "Yes, but did you hear the other side of the story," when in reality there are more likely twenty sides to the average story rather than only two. This mentality considers a man either a sinner or a saint rather than understanding that there is something of the sinner and the saint in every man. The young religious has the delusion that if she is not yet a saint she soon will be, only to learn to her subsequent discouragement how far away is "soon." The sacrament of penance is not for the sinless but for the sinful soul. It is as useless for the saint as it is for the soul perverse in evil. The one has no matter for the sacrament and the other has no will for it. The problem of the good nun and confession is in seeing herself for what she is. She flutters between the tendency to make sins out of nothing and the tendency to make nothing out of sin. Honesty and objectivity outline the happy medium of virtue. Every woman fluctuates between depression and elation. Depressed, a world of guilt lies on the shoulders of the nun; elated, she dons the innocence of an angel.

The common exaggeration of purity of motive does not help this situation. Complex man is incapable of a pure motive; his motives will always be multiple. He will never have the pure goodness to avoid gratification in the punishment of an enemy or the pure viciousness to avoid some regret at trampling those in the way of his own satisfaction. The honest religious sees her uncharitableness but has the courage to make her criticism because she believes it is required of her, regardless of the harsh judgment which will be passed on her. The "virtuous" nun who abstains from criticism because "it is not right" seldom adverts to her fears of the disapproval of those criticized or corrected. The nun must understand that all her motives are mixed and that God alone can judge her guilt. Her actions are no more perfect than she is perfect and no more sinful than she is sinful. The religious who sees her poverty in the riches of God, and her ugliness in the beauty of God, her falsity in the truth of God, her selfishness in the love of God will have no trouble finding sufficient material for confession, nor will she make confession an occasion for the edification of her director.

Trust in God allows the penitent to escape the predicament of the sinner who is never sure she committed sin. This nun, instead of living her life fruitfully, wastes her time picking through the wrinkles of her soul to see what she can find. She is like the woman hiding a blanket from the moths when she should be using it to keep warm. She is like the little girl who heard herself so often cautioned, "Nice little girls don't do that," that she grew up without the slightest idea of what nice little girls did do. There is no place so revealing of the mature religious as the confessional. She never lets it make a useless introvert of her, or permits it to make her a spiritual automaton with a vending-machine mentality on grace.

The subject of confession cannot be dealt with unless something is said of the human being on the other side of the grille. As has been said, every religious wants a holy and learned director, for such help as he can provide is invaluable. But she must not let the wish be father to the thought and consider the confessor holy because she wishes he were so. The holiness of anyone is well beyond the competence of most enlightened people to judge. Often the nun's admiration for the director's spirituality comes from his high opinion of the penitent. And so it goes when simplicity, honesty, and the love of God are not great. Just as many nuns go through the motions of prayer without praying, so many directors go through the motions of direction without directing. The wise spiritual director tries to keep out of the way of the Holy Spirit, and the wise nun never lets the director replace the Holy Spirit in her life.

But when there is real spiritual direction available it should never be passed by or wasted. The wise nun never gives up her watch for direction for it is one of the sure roads to prayer, holiness, and God. But her search is never frantic or her need exaggerated, for she never loses sight of the fact that God is in the boat despite its pitchings and tossings. God does not need a spiritual director to help in His guidance of souls. It is the souls who need the director. Many a nun, because she can sit down and write a letter to a director and receive an answer in return, acts as if God were powerless to communicate directly with her. If God does not seem to be doing so it is because the soul is not open to the message. Both God and the soul being spiritual, the thrill of contact is not registered and may go unnoticed. If a spiritual director can be helpful how much more helpful is Almighty God whose communication with the soul only ceases when the soul's door is closed against Him. At such times a spiritual director is of the greatest value in pointing out what has happened. Through his advice she can turn again to God, opening her soul to Him. It is the work of the director to work with that soul to show her just how many obstacles there are in the way of the opening door, and to help her to remove them as soon as possible.

For the same reason that God chose men for the ministry of forgiveness he chose them for spiritual direction of souls. It is important that the soul be not above seeking the help that God thus provides. Naaman's contempt for the water of the river Jordan almost left him a leper for life. It is even more important that superiors do not deprive their subjects of the help available to them from spiritual direction. Strange as it all may seem and despite the clarity of Church Law on the matter, few religious are well instructed in the freedom they have to seek the spiritual direction they alone can judge they need. No superior is permitted to refuse a subject permission to see a priest for peace of conscience or better progress in the way of God. The bishop alone grants permission for any priest in good standing to answer any such petition for help, nor can he or the superior inquire into the reasons such help is sought. Yet there are those who consider their authority violated if they are not permitted to sit in judgment on the conditions giving rise to such a request for help and guidance.

The freedom of conscience of the individual religious can never be violated, which should be obvious to all for even God does not presume to do it. Freedom of conscience was His idea in the first place; religious should not be the ones to doubt the wisdom of it. So jealous are some superiors of their position or authority that without any sense of wrongness they will insist that a nun is too young to see a priest alone. If she really cannot, it is not lack of years but lack of virtue which makes it so. Such an attitude may be warranted, but if it is, it does not say much for the virtue of the priest either. It is a strange thing that a nun could be considered old enough to make a vow she is apparently too young to keep. It would be a strange rectory or religious house in which no one was ever allowed to see a priest alone. The sacredness of privacy is respected by all the professions, in every country in which there is freedom. Surely it should be respected in the Church. When it is not, it is an open admission that the Church has done its work very badly.

Something must be said about written conscience matter. The rules for such are not very explicit but they are very implicit. Canon Law does not explicitly permit such letters to be written to confessors or directors. However, it does explicitly forbid any superior under severe penalties to force a manifestation of conscience. Therefore, who but the blindest of the blind could not see that there is no difference between demanding that a subject reveal something and taking and opening a letter which she has clearly marked and sealed as conscience matter. If any honorable person went into the cell of another and saw a slip of paper on which was written "Conscience Matter" she would not think of reading it. If she did so she would commit sin. If a superior has serious reason to believe that a nun is using this device for her own private Lonely Hearts' Club, the matter should be taken up with her formally. The world has a lot of space ready for such people; the convent should have none. If a nun can be kept from normal opportunities to better her spiritual life, the only reason for her to be where she is, then there is a serious structural weakness in religious life as it operates.

The nun wishing to write conscience matter — and this should be done sparingly and prudently — is free to do so. She simply writes the letter and seals it in an envelope marked "Conscience Matter" which she puts in another envelope and sends out through the superior. The superior is never permitted to open such a letter or inquire why it was written or what it dealt with. Let it be faced, there are many nuns who do not trust their superiors to leave such letters unopened. When such a judgment has real foundation in fact, and the superior either through ignorance or defect of character cannot be trusted to so deal with such letters, religious are free to send such letters without the superior's clearance or permission, provided there is a legitimate and reasonable need, and scandal is avoided in doing so. When a conscientious nun has to do such a thing it is evident that her superior has so lost the confidence of her sisters that she were better removed. Women are often distrustful of other women, but when nuns are right in being so, there can be nothing very praiseworthy in the religious life they see.

Still, because prejudice is and must always be in favor of authority, and insubordination to any degree should never be encouraged, much wisdom must be used in such cases. But there is no wisdom in denying that they exist, or refusing to look into them when one plainly has the duty to do so. Through all such discussion it must be remembered that union of the soul with God underlies this matter; it would be unbelievable that the finest souls in the world were not to be trusted to be conscientious, the existence of Judas notwithstanding.

While the practice of penance in itself does not seem to be directly connected with the sacrament, still it is, because the only reason for penance is sin. Since there is sin in the world there must be penance. This is the reason underlying fasting, abstinence, Lenten and Advent regulations, the forbidding of marriage during the closed seasons. These represent the public penances of the Church. Private penance also is highly recommended. And every director is asked by some of those religious he directs about the advisability of, or permission for, corporal penances above and beyond the ordinary ones. Most directors consider these the last outposts of direction; but some fail to see that extraordinary rashness underlies many requests for permission, and extraordinary wisdom explains the few permissions that are ever given. Seldom does a director see in the penitent seeking this permission the full use of the more important facilities for virtue in her daily life, which would warrant him permitting something over and above. It is an extraordinary thing being sought when so many ordinary obligations are ignored, unfulfilled, or done halfheartedly. There is a great deal of corporal penance in community life itself, the daily association of temperaments and dispositions so foreign to each other. A soul must have reached great heights to have accepted her obligations and the enervating chores of un-relenting dedication without murmur. The charity required for peaceful coexistence is of an ineffably higher order than the spirit needed for corporal penances which so easily en-courage delusions and originate in misguided zeal. It is ridiculous to have nuns further obligating themselves when present obligations have not been well handled, or when dispensations from more fundamental ones are being sought because of nervous exhaustion or physical debility. No one can say there is no room for corporal penances in modern religious life, but the findings of psychiatry and the new awareness of mental instability make second thought im-perative before they can be encouraged or permitted. Certainly they could never be considered where the penitent is not accepting the normal limitations of the body and the minor and major sicknesses which are the lot of every human stumbling across the line of middle age. Sickness is a great form of penance which few have the mental acumen to turn to profit.

A book on sickness in religious life would fill a real need. But while awaiting it some conclusions can be reached. The silence and solitude of religious life is designed for closer contact with Almighty God. In times of sickness there is great danger that it will be used to concentrate on one's own miseries. When this is done the miseries are magnified and last longer than they normally would. A fever-ish night, alone, with sleep impossible, makes hours out of minutes. Nor should those fortunately blessed with good health consider that it is all a matter of imagination rather than real suffering. Doctors have told people their sicknesses were imaginary only to find some patients had imagined themselves to death. Still religious in sickness cannot resort to the harried occupations which make their normal days fly, and they do not have the interests, occupations, or obligations which distract many people from themselves and their woes. Modern religious, too, are victims of modern advertising which inclines people to believe there is no reason to suffer pain as if it were not a part of life, and much of it is to be endured with patience. They often lack the judgment to know whether it is a virtue to endure the inevitable or to make their suffering plain to responsible superiors so that later and more serious illness can be avoided. It is a challenge to the religious suffering pain in the age of aspirins and other drugs to banish thoughts of self to the extent required for heroic virtue.

Few religious want to be neurotics but many are. They haunt the doctors' offices. Some doctors, lacking the good judgment or patience every good doctor wishes he had, consider almost any religious coming to see them to be neurotic. Some of them err, and some forget that they have contributed a good deal to the making of these neurotics. First, some of these doctors do not have the humility to admit their limitations. Because some patients extend to them the admiration and dependence that should be reserved for God, some doctors don't appreciate how ridiculous the comparison really is. Being a little like God, it is hard for them to tell the patient candidly that there is nothing more they can do for her. Instead they carry these patients along indefinitely as part of their charity load. It takes a little more charity, however, to tell a religious patient that her affliction is one she will have to endure because he does not know what to do about it. It is too easy to call them neurotics and let it go at that. Doctors should be very careful in calling anyone a neurotic, let alone religious, because many autopsies have proven how wrong they have been. It takes courage to tell a religious that she may or may not be a neurotic when the tests reveal nothing that can be dealt with. That does not mean that there is no suffering, for few now doubt the reality of the pains of the neurotic. But it does mean that the doctor can save himself and the patient much wasted time by not having her coming back for useless treatments.

It is sad to see religious, who should have a deep love for truth, being given sterile hypos because they cannot sleep without an injection, or taking drugs not only for imagined pain, but because they are afraid they might have a pain if they don't take a pill of some sort. Despite all the wild talk of wiping sickness out, and the reports of all that has been accomplished in conquering illness — and this should not be underestimated — pain is a necessary part of life, and religious should be able to make a slightly better job than the common man of accepting it with little notice and minimum complaint. Many religious are neurotics, but not because they are religious. They are neurotics because they are people and many people are neurotics; religious life has its share of them. A factor making it impossible to eliminate them from the cloisters is the entry of candidates in their youth where there is usually the least evidence of neuroticism. They are in their physical prime, enthusiastic, distracted from the present by anticipation of their future in religion, many of them even anxious that physical defects not be found to keep them home. They are less concerned with themselves physically than at any other time in their lives. And they have not yet borne the burdens of religion or experienced the ennui of unrewarding labor. They have great good will about foregoing the blessings of the married state, a home of their own and children, the privilege of leaving the job in the evening and coming back to it in the morning from another world. But given a few years of the uphill struggle it takes to overcome herself, and slowly the traits of the neurotic appear, most of them to remain for life. Here is where the blessing of any community is the honest neurotic who sees her state and makes the best of it. There is no panacea for neuroticism, but the willingness to live religious life to the fullest possible extent, with as little consideration for self as is reconcilable with intelligence and good judgment, will do more to control and manage it than anything else. The sufferings of the neurotic are no less real simply because they are largely homemade.

Religious are far too inclined to consider the good Catholic who is a doctor to be a good doctor too. The Catholic who is also a good doctor is inclined to consider the patient more religious than patient, and through misguided kindness to let her use her complaints to vitiate her responsibility unnecessarily. It is bad for a doctor to accuse a religious of unjustly malingering, but it is just as bad to encourage in her any oversolicitude for the body. Sickness is part of life, and a most acceptable form of penance, although one's sickness should never become penance for the whole community. As such it is worthy of acceptance and endurance as much as it is of treatment. When it is not quite clear which it deserves there is plenty of worthwhile guidance available to religious in the matter. The stupidity of reporting every little indisposition is only matched by the stupidity of greater consequence, guarding the secret of one's health as if it were more important than the latest formula for jet propulsion.

18. The Apostolate

THE zealous nun in the active community longs for the hours of prayer, her source of strength. And rare is the zealous nun in the cloister who does not long to go into the world and conquer it for Christ. This indicates that the spiritual life and the apostolate are inseparable. The religious enters the convent for her own salvation, but she is also concerned with the salvation of others. The Incarnation is meaningless without the Redemption. To consider Christ becoming Man without thinking of Christ dying for man is blindness. While the crucifix evokes sentiments of love for and gratitude to God it is essentially the symbol of the apostolate. As surely as the crucifix impresses a man with the necessity of man loving God, it must also impress him with the fact of God actually loving man and desiring his salvation. Therefore anyone loving God must add his own desires to those of Christ dying for the salvation of souls. "If any man says he loves God and hates his neighbor, the same is a liar," says St. John. The loving ascent of the mind and heart to embrace God must include a branching out of this love to embrace one's fellowman. The upright timber of the Cross lifts the soul to God and the extended arms take it to its neighbor.

Zeal comes from the love of the soul for God. Identity of the will with the will of God demands zeal for souls.

Just as the apostolate cannot be fruitful without the love of God, neither can the love of God be real without the apostolate. When the administration of a community is not concerned about the apostolate its condition is deplorable. Those who would insist the security of the soul lies in being close to God lose sight of the fact that there is no security in running away from the people. Security comes from the love of God which demands going out to the people.

Religious have been reared on the rule. Its infraction is considered worse than sin despite the fact that theologians have taught the contrary. Sin can only enter where there is contempt for the rule. Charity has become secondary to the rule. This cannot be, for the rule is not God, but God is Charity. Charity is above the rule, and the rule is useless without it. Any fear of downgrading the rule comes from fear of abuses creeping in, as if there were anything for an abuse to creep into where there is not charity. But charity governs the apostolate, and this has been proven by every missionary endeavor of the Church. With charity there is success; without it there is failure. The guiding principle of the successful missionary is charity, the love of God through which he seeks every occasion to help his people. Women find a different spirit in religious returning from their missions. Some consider it a dangerous independence but in reality it is the result of being guided in their work by zeal for souls rather than the rule. Certainly the religious without tremendous respect for the rule is not fit to be a missionary, but no rule can actually take precedence over the good of souls. If it did it would have to take precedence over Redemption.

This is a frightening concept. But what can be more

frightening than for a man or woman to have one life in which to prove his or her love for God or suffer hell for eternity? There is no place in the apostolate for playing it safe, there is only room for the charity of Christ urging one on to the sacrifices necessary, trusting in the help of God to survive any difficulty arising, even the apparently insurmountable. Christ's charter to the Apostles did not die with them, nor is He any less truly present with His apostles of today.

Many features of the apostolate must be rethought when so much of the Church seems a myth hidden under the shell of statistics, compiled from wishful thinking or the desire to please authority. Glory in numbers is the poorest prop for authority. The fact that the great encyclicals on social justice came from the popes does not hide the fact of social injustice supported by Catholic authorities in Catholic institutions. Many of the historic works have so changed that only the vestiges remain of what was once the purest evidence of Christian charity. It is the obligation of the individual religious to determine for herself what the apostolate means and to use every legitimate means to engage in it. Nor can the interpretation of the constitution of her order or society, in which it seems she has been trained to take so little personal interest, relieve her of the personal responsibility she has to God and souls. It should never have been left to Protestant missionaries to stimulate Catholic apostolic endeavor in Latin America; but it was. Many wonderful works begun under the inspiration of God and the zeal of holy men and women have degenerated into means of support and prestige for religious orders. Hospitals founded as works of charity have become institutions of business where the community earns the money to support itself, and religious are too busy with the cash registers to attend the patients. Educational institutions have sprung from this same source only to become self-sustaining competitors of the state-endowed university, no longer willing or able to take in the needy and deserving.

This state of affairs has been due to a socio-religious evolution almost imperceptible in its progress until now. The clock cannot be turned back nor can responsibilities legitimately assumed and obligations prudently undertaken be repudiated. But provision must be made to direct the labors of religious into more apostolic fields, to fill the more basic needs of men in relation to their God. This can never be left to the zeal of an order or religious society, for orders or societies have no more zeal than the members themselves.

There is no provision in the economy of grace for a sacrament receivable by an order, nor are actual graces given to corporate bodies. If the demands of charity are not met there is the deterioration of religion, and an uninspiring coldness in the lives of religious. This may be the reason individual nuns are rebuked for talking to "seculars" on the street, as if there were some strange contamination in dealing with the same people from which the vocations came in the first place. Many nuns are not permitted to eat in the homes of their own parents as if it were no longer a fit place for the consecrated virgin of the family. Others are marched like the proverbial chain gang from the convent to the parish church, forbidden to break ranks to speak with a lay person regardless of the need, as if for fear they might escape. The calm mien and bowed head are perhaps intended to convey the idea that there is nothing on the mind of the religious but the act of homage she is about to offer God in the Mass, but oftener than not it conveys the idea of disinterest.

Through this formality the best opportunities are missed to discuss their mutual problems, problems of their children in the school or home. The laity who support the nuns are deserving of at least their passing interest. Nuns in mission countries would be useless if they did not take advantage of almost every occasion to talk to the people in the hope of awakening their interest in God and the Church.

When contact with the laity is made an occasion of sin it is open admission that the religious has not the conviction she needs to remain where she is. Anything can be made an occasion of sin, but if the religious who have been trained in the love of God and feasted on the sacraments cannot mix with the laity in the name of God, then who can? The normal untrained lay person in the world takes such contacts as a part of her life and does not perish for them, or even consider her salvation seriously jeopardized. Religious make a virtue out of the very opposite thing Christ urged His Apostles to do, go out into the country and bring in the harvest of souls. The nun who does not love God will certainly forsake Him whether she be confined to barracks or remain in the strictest enclosure. The rule of life which excludes charity or reduces it to the minimum ultimately produces a sterile form of spirituality so unrewarding that it will have largely lost its appeal even for those sincerely wishing to love God.

Religious in the apostolate have only one thing to offer mankind, the living proof of the power of grace in man. To show forth that grace they must be willing to go among men with the virtue they should have by reason of their years of dedication. The apostolate is the glory of the Church, the only real proof of its vitality. Where there is no apostolate there is no vitality. Today, the Holy Father, understanding that the spiritual starvation of the masses is much more extensive than physical starvation, has demanded that religious show this power. He wants men to return to hope in God for all that matters, rather than depend on the elusive heaven on earth promised by the false phophets of materialism.

The very thought of lifting many of the restrictions on religious creates dismay in the hearts of thoughtful superiors, as well it may. But this dismay is evidence enough that religious for all their years in convents have not acquired the virtue needed to assure their faithful service to God without severe restriction. Who will say that this makes much of an ideal of union with God, or promises much joy from a union that appears to be little more than an endurance contest?

Certainly no religious is fit for the apostolate unless she has a deep love for God and enough virtue to cleave to God in the face of the temptations that freedom offers in the modern world. Certainly the one lesson the world needs is that a man or woman can be faithful to God under any conditions where love for God is real. The only other thing needed for fidelity under such conditions is the grace of God which will never be wanting to those who serve Him.

19. Conclusion

RELIGIOUS life is like a journey by sail across a sea into the arms of God. There are obvious problems in this journey, and others less obvious but more important. For the one without a boat the journey seems clearly impossible. But given boat and sail, and put on a raging sea, the same one will wish she had never seen either boat or sail for her very life itself is threatened; and it seemed so secure when she was standing on the shore.

Religious life is not only boat and sail; it is the very best possible boat and sail for the journey. But there are other factors too. There is the wind of grace always blowing in the direction of God. There is the course to be arranged for the most lift to fill the highest quantity of sail. The job of the nun is to sail the course and control the tiller so that there is no obstacle to the wind of grace filling her sails to the utmost. How human to go off course, to lose sight of the destination, to stop for something momentarily more attractive, to reef the sails to see what passing pleasure can be fished out of the depths of the unknown, to let the sail lines be scraped thin on the edge of carelessness. These things all slow the trip and distract the sailor from her purpose, make the destination seem more unattainable, and expose her to the danger of being lost enroute through

221

stupidity, laxity, independence, or indifference. The motto of the nun should be, "Sail on, sail on." According to her eager interest she will study the course, improve her technique, cast distraction aside, and stick to her work. With the wind of grace filling the sails, there will be power for the roughest seas and the stormiest weather.

In the beginning of this book the religious was asked to keep before her the Sacred Face of the suffering Christ. Every nun has been called, and has considered herself, a spouse of Christ. Surely this is a figure of speech, but it is used because the union between any soul and God cannot properly be described even by the deepest, truest, clearest, most forceful, and entrancing language. Since there are not words to describe the union of the soul and God, those have to be used which describe the most glorious union any human being could imagine, that between the most wonderful of men and the most wonderful of women. But this must be done with the knowledge that such a picture multiplied by infinity would just barely express the beginning of the happiness of union with Perfection, who is God. The religious is not the only spouse of God, for this union is open to any soul. It is just that the term seems more apt when applied to the woman professing union with God in this world, gladly passing over the lesser union permitted her. So the nun rejoices in her title, metaphorical though it be. And although some of the old-timers in religion may smile at the joy of the young nun in this figure of speech, because they know how easily its significance may be lost later on, the smile goes with a prayer that she will never learn how cruel life really is. What the prayer really means to express is the hope that no matter how cruel life may be, the young nun will always have the courage to meet it, neither bending nor breaking, but sailing on.

If the nun is not a spouse of Christ, it is only because she is more than that. For spouse cannot in any way describe the role of one in whom Christ really lives and who really lives in Christ. The firmest marriage union leaves each spouse with a sense of frustration that their oneness is not more surely attainable. Union with Christ leads to the eternal oblivion of anything but the joy and happiness of being one with Almighty God Himself.

If the earthly "spouse of Christ" must come back to reality, it is only because she has rejoiced more in the title than in the role. She has forgotten her unworthiness. In her joy for herself she has forgotten her Spouse. She does forget her spouse when the crushed, crowned, crucified Christ is out of mind and she fails to make His life her own.

She must go back to the Passion of Christ and ask herself, "If He is really God, why was He arrested? If He really had twelve legions of angels at His disposal why did they not come to His defense?" Only faith can tell her that there are reasonable answers to these questions. Unless she is afraid of the cost of loving Christ, as His Apostles were in His critical hour, she will find the answers to these questions by searching for them in the Passion of Christ. It is a lifetime's work which no one else can do for her. No book can tell her what they are; no one can force her eyes to see them. She must do these things herself. Only when she does will religious life mean anything to her, will her longest days seem all too short for what must be done, will her sorest trials seem trivial, will she always feel unworthy of the calling that is hers, and staggered by the love of the One who calls her to it. She will never be worthy of it; she never could be worthy of it. Only the person foolish enough to forget this will consider religious life unrewarding; all others must know it is too short a time to prepare for a union so far above a human being that only God could think of it.